AF600806

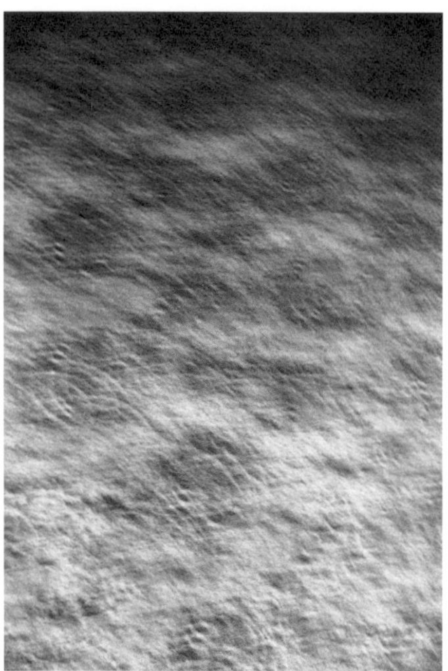

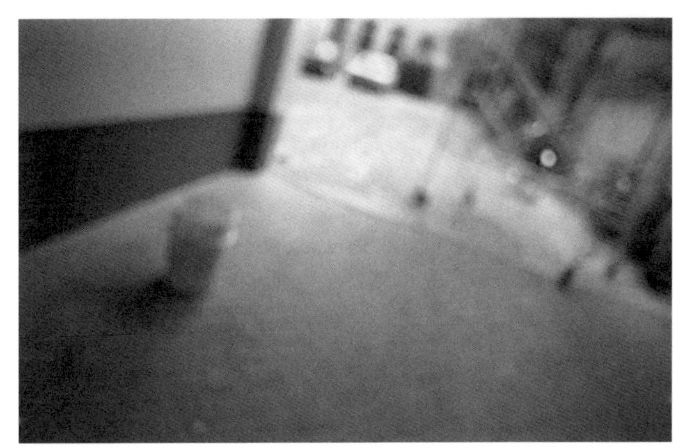

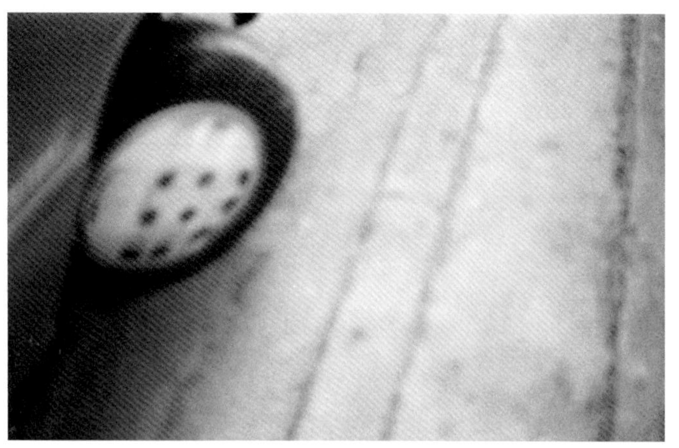

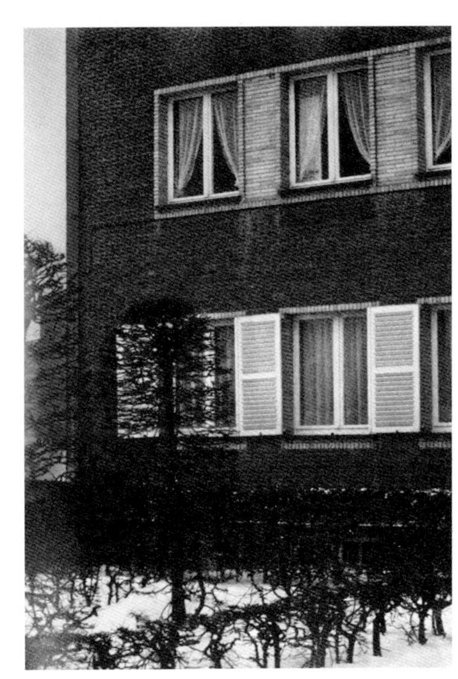

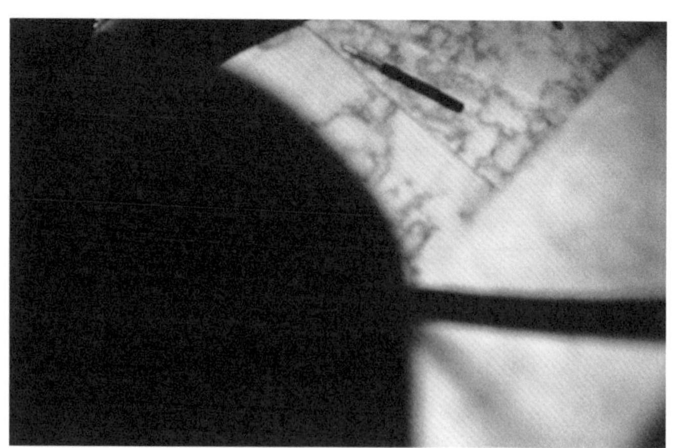

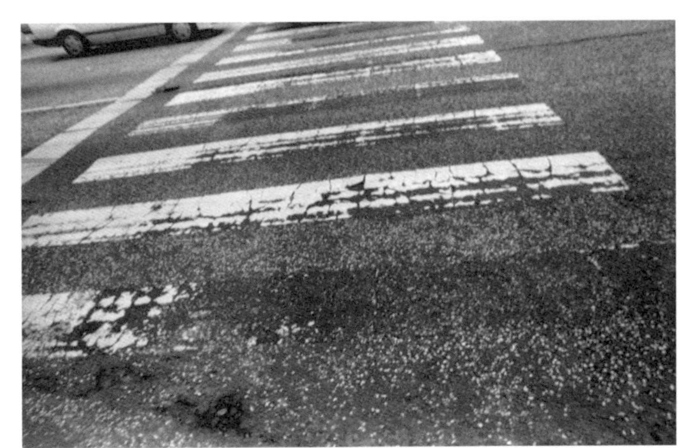

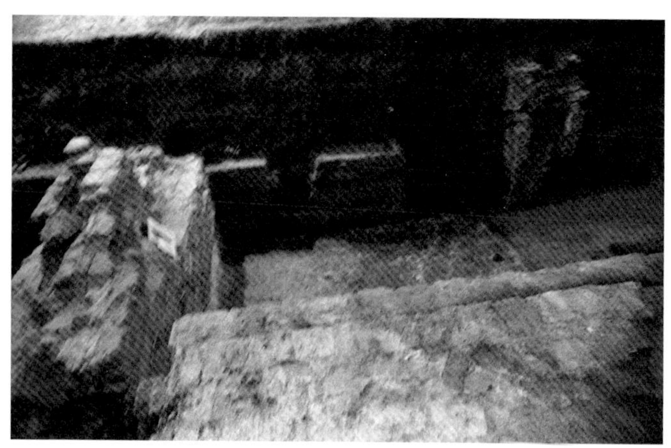

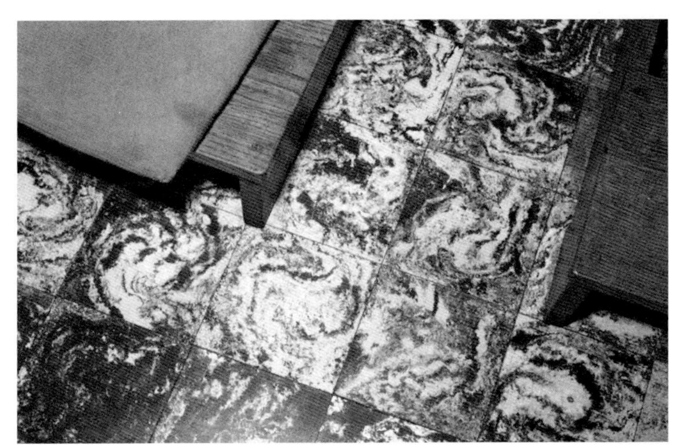

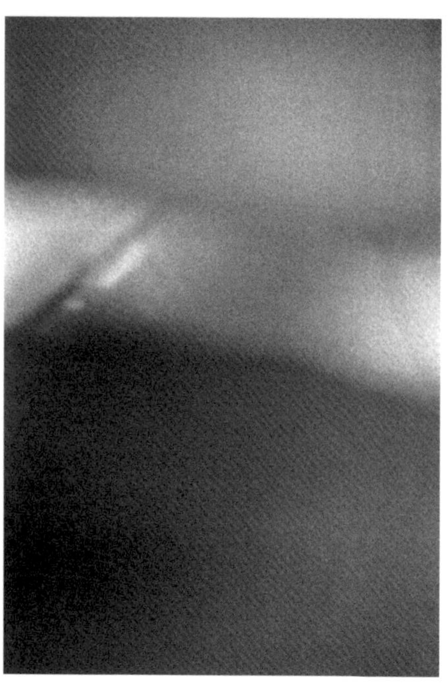

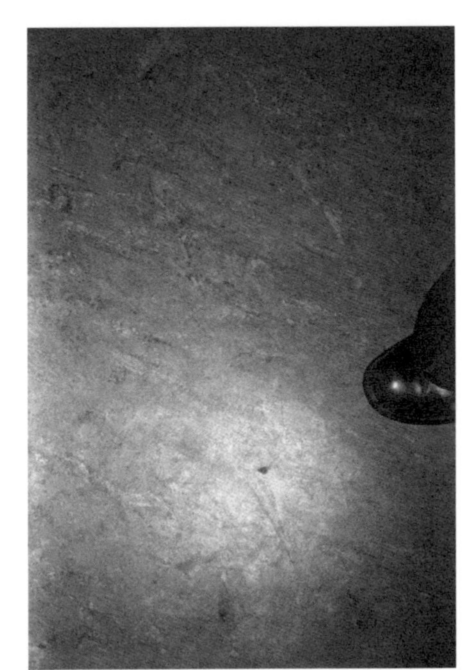

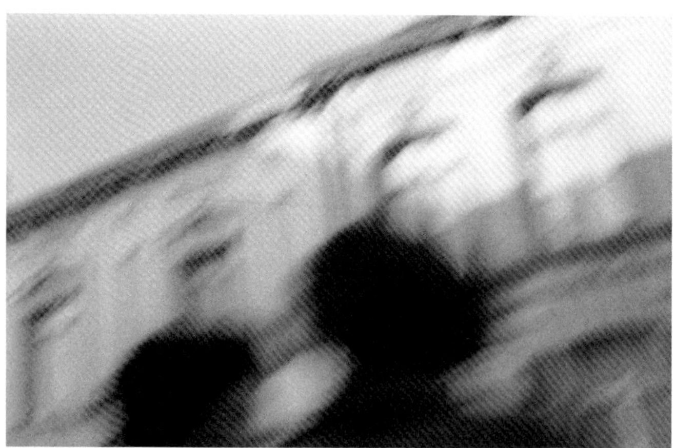

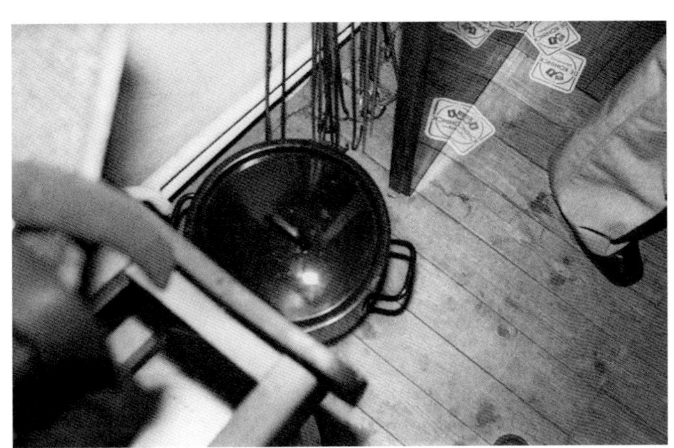

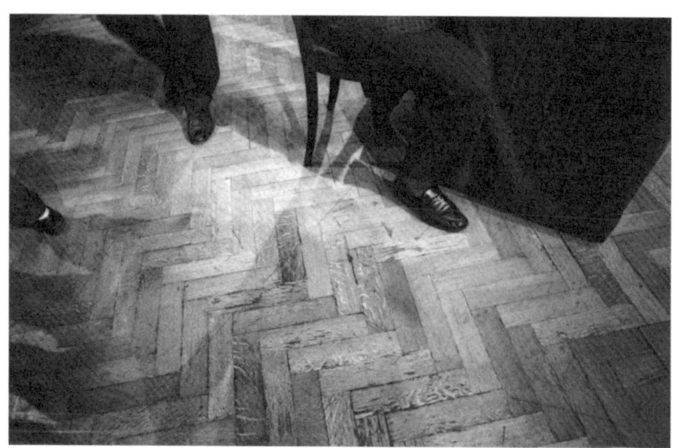

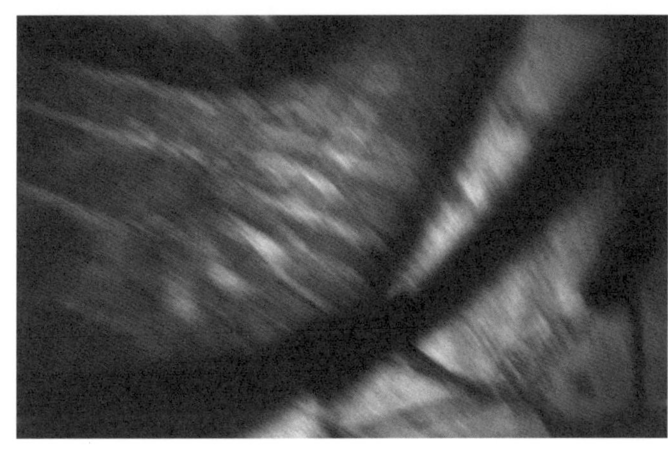

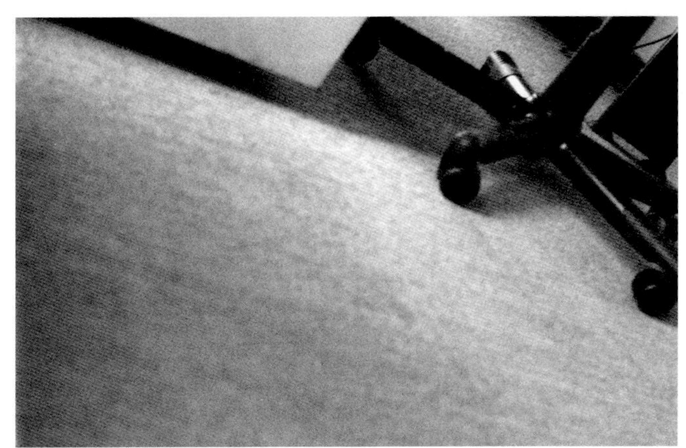

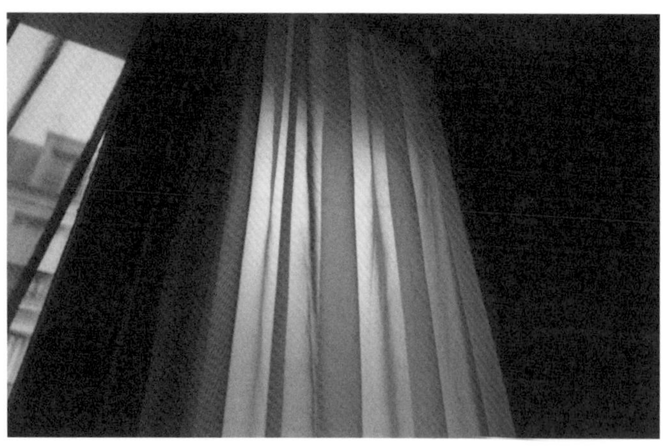

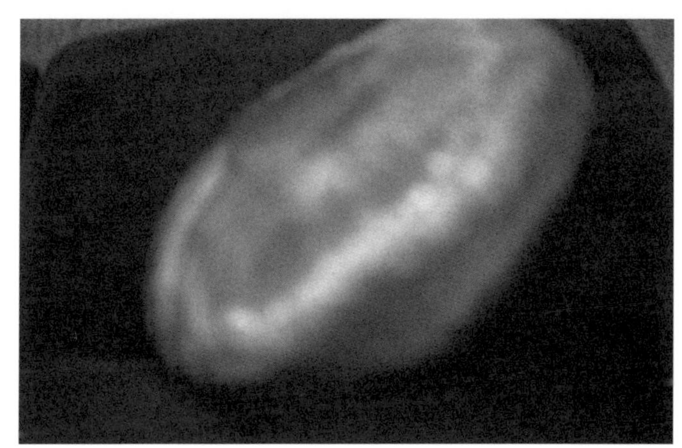

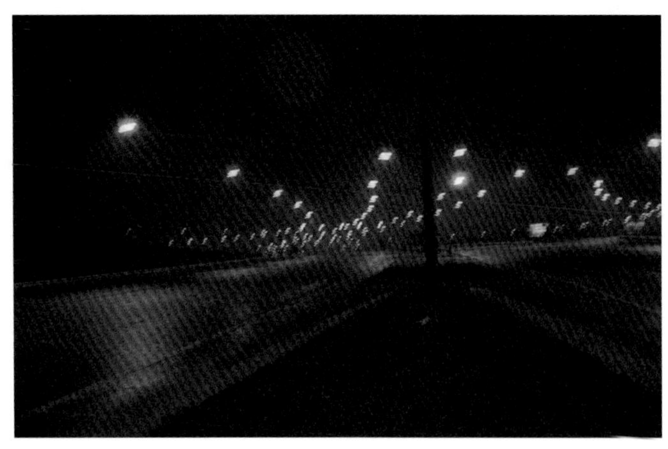

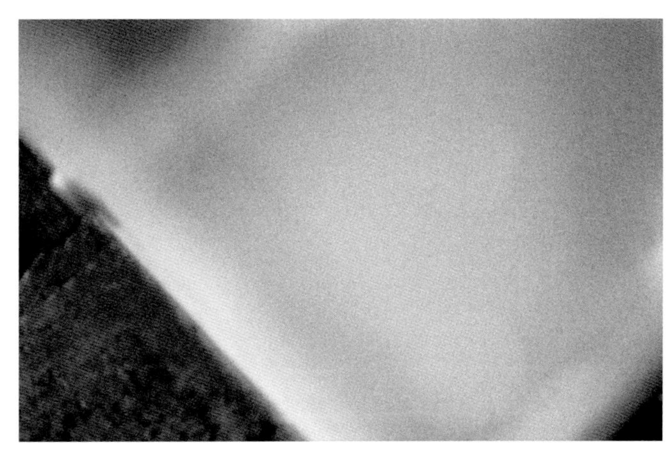

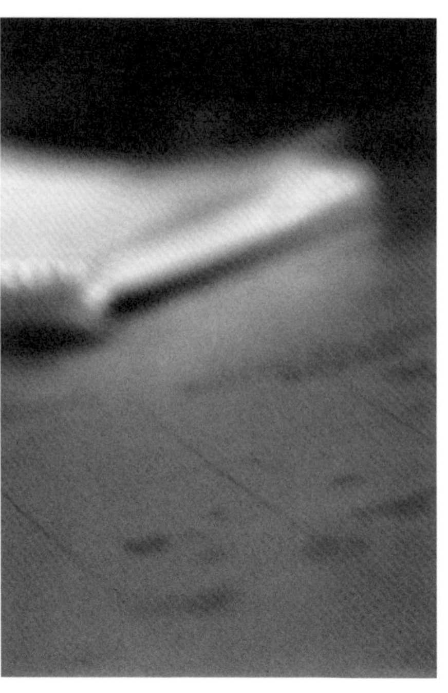

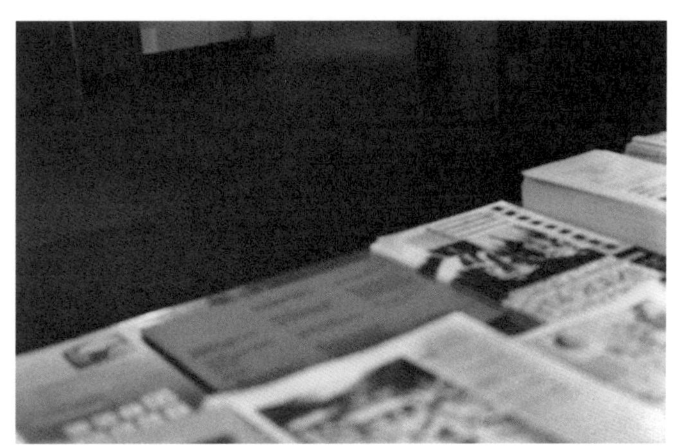

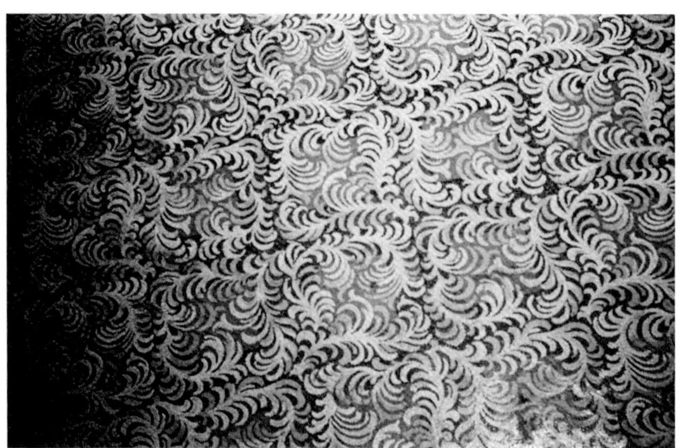

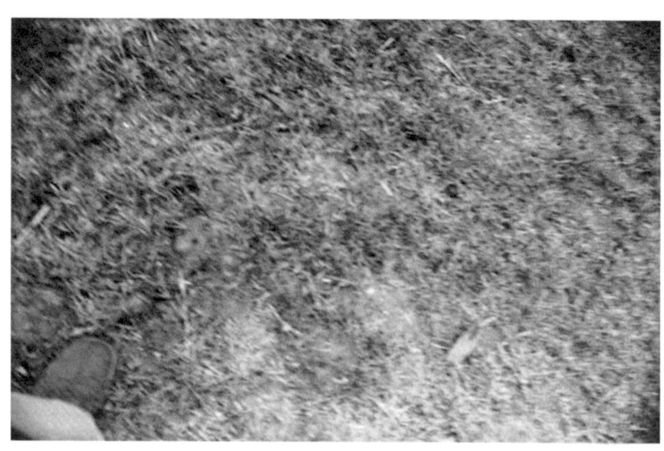

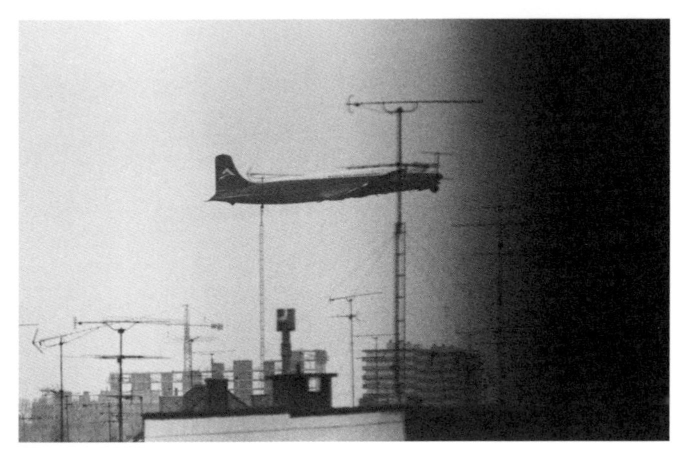

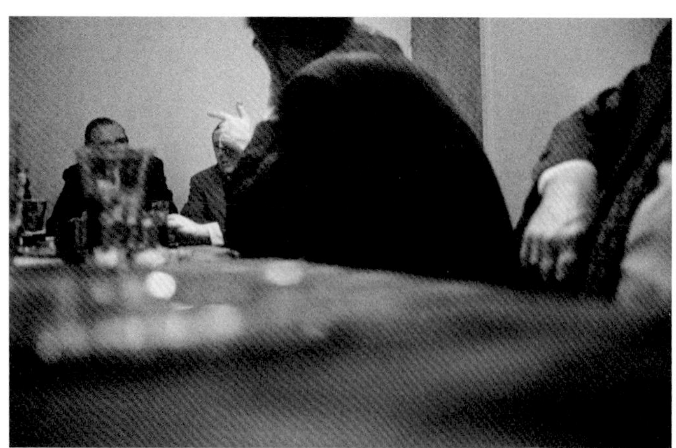

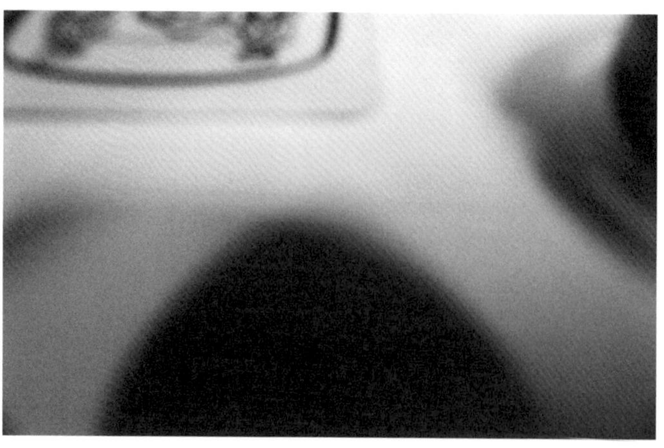

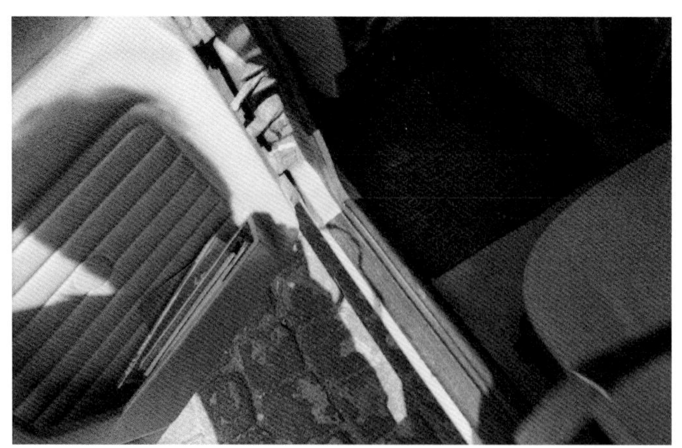

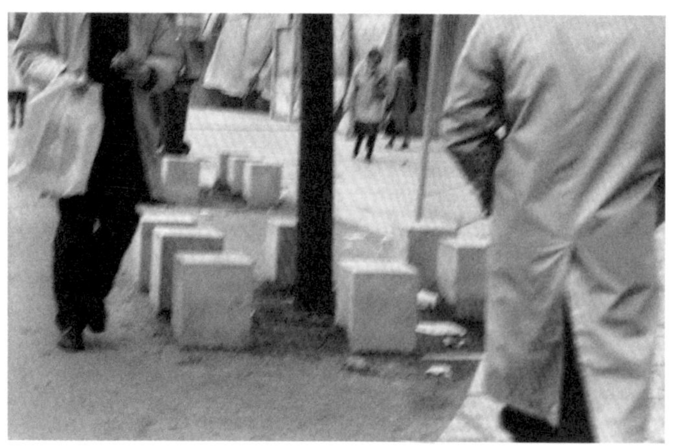

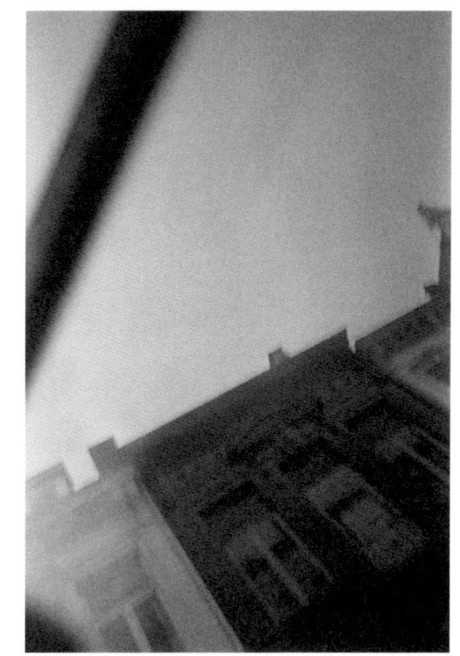

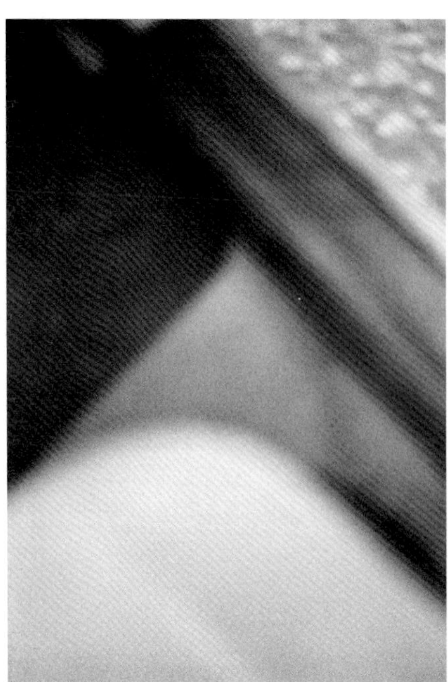

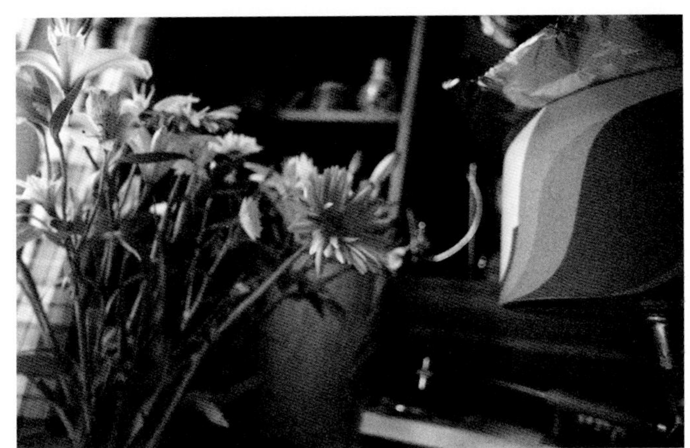

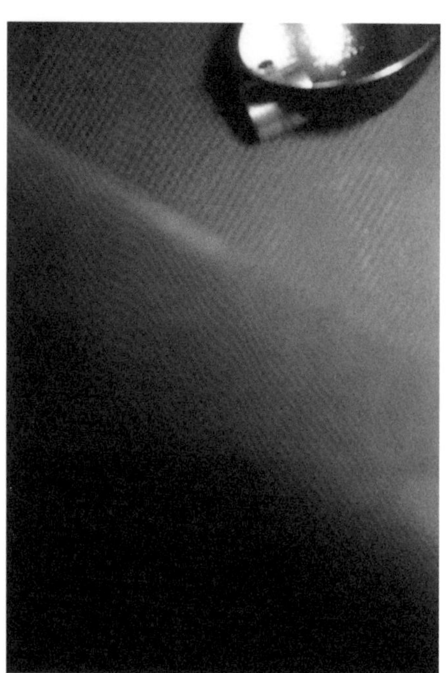

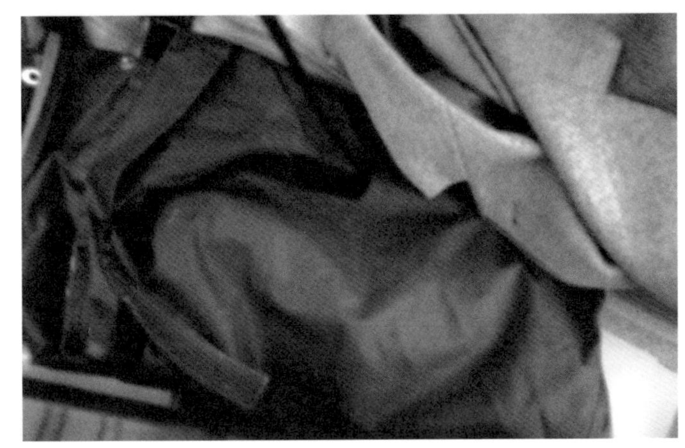

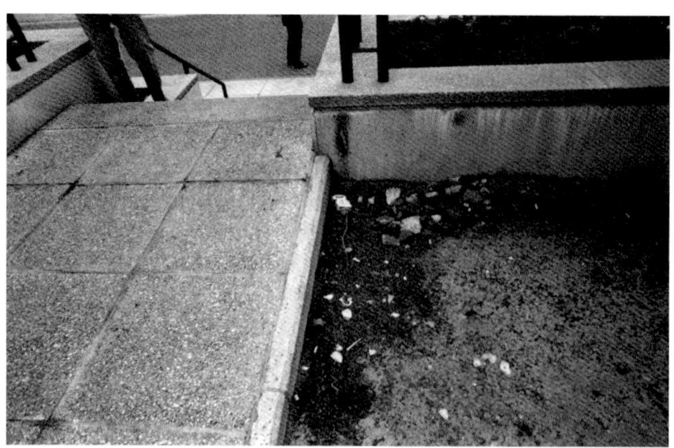

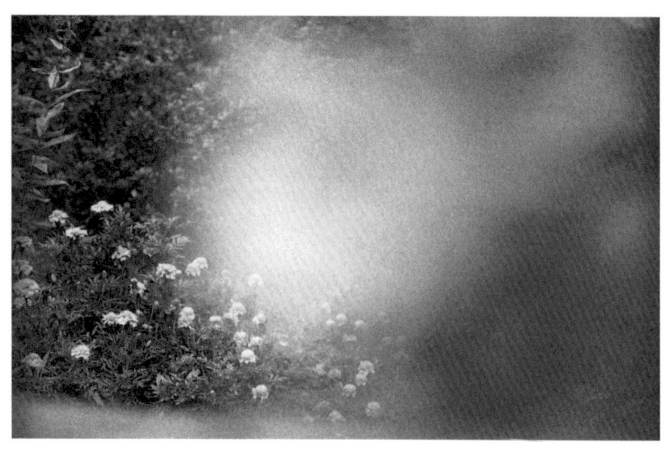

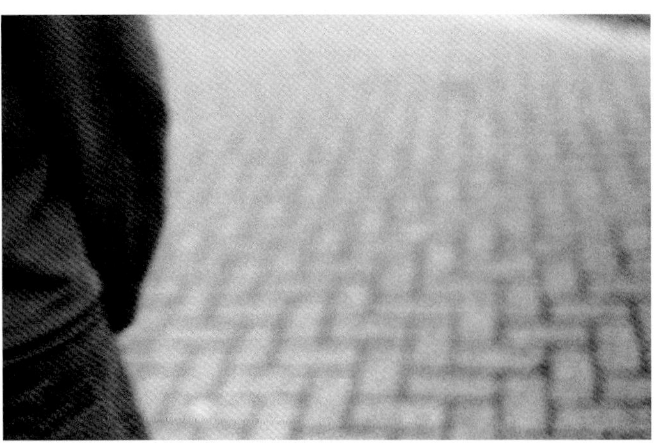

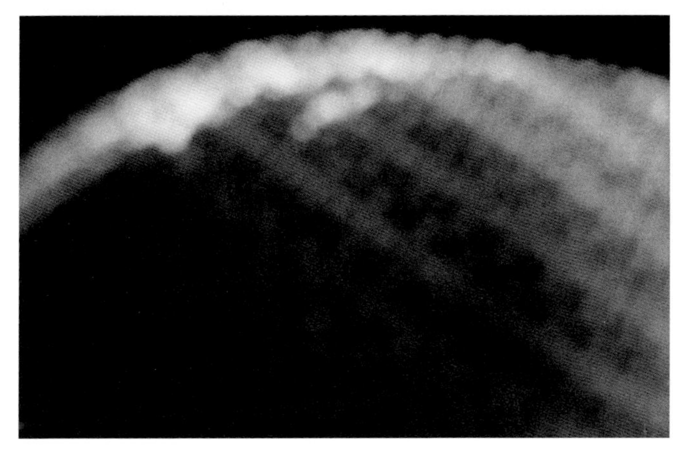

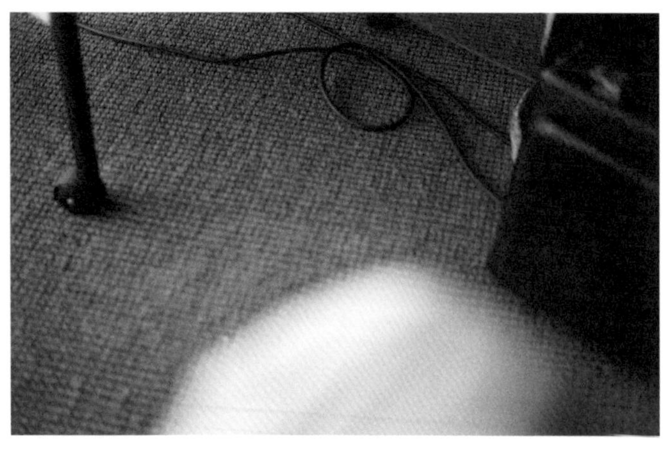

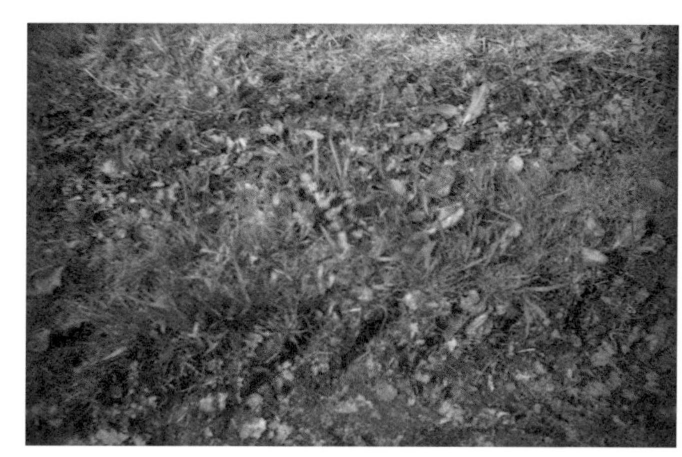

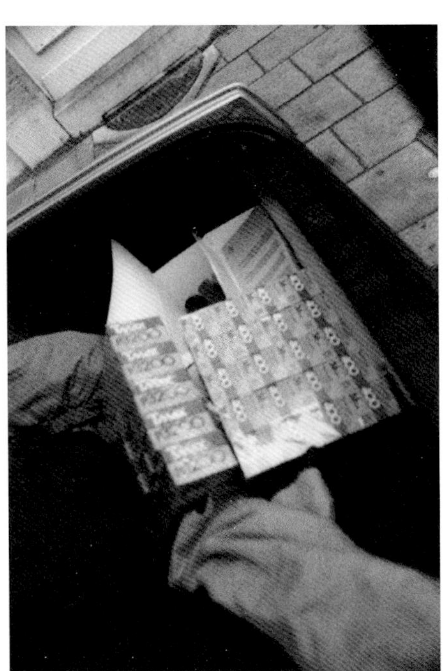

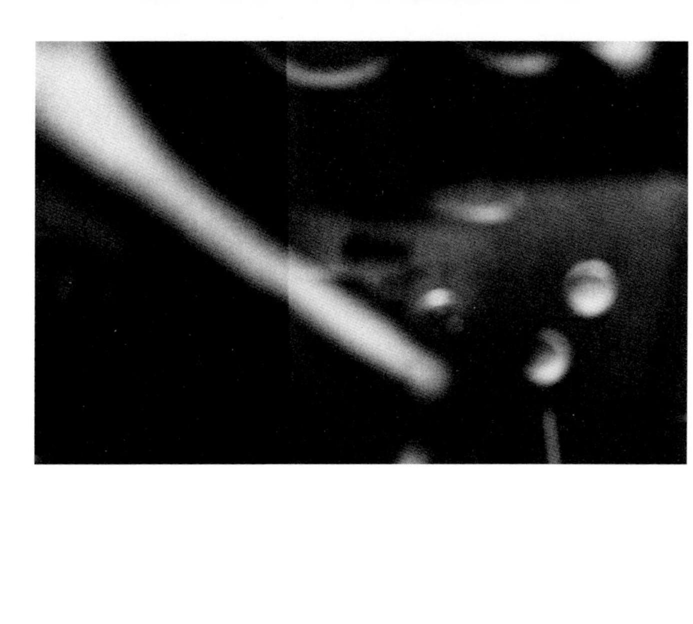

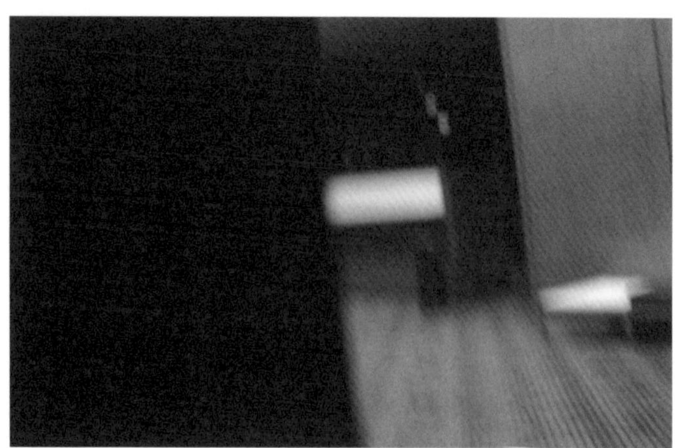

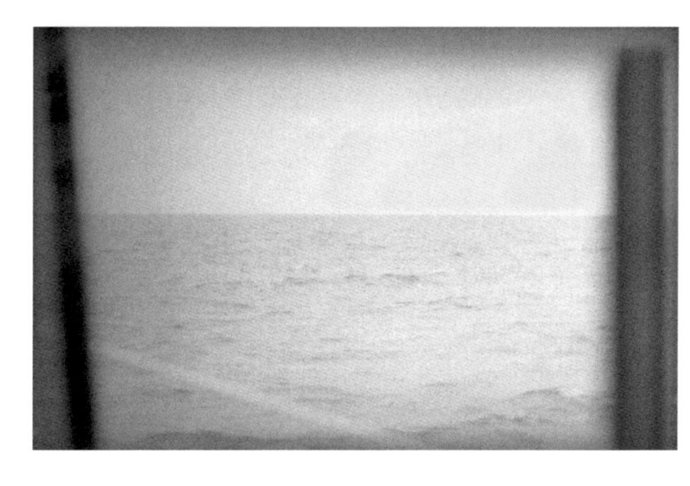

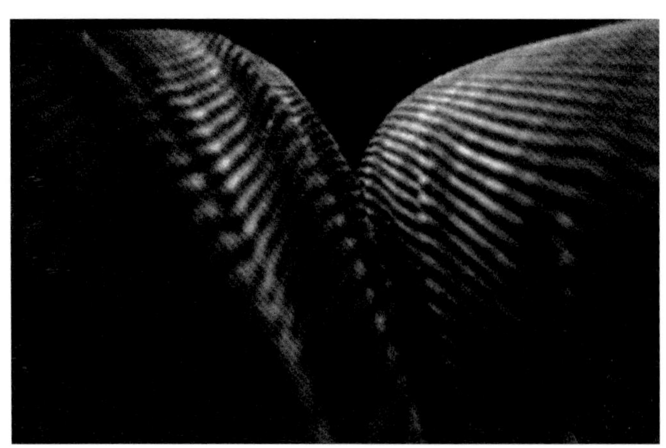

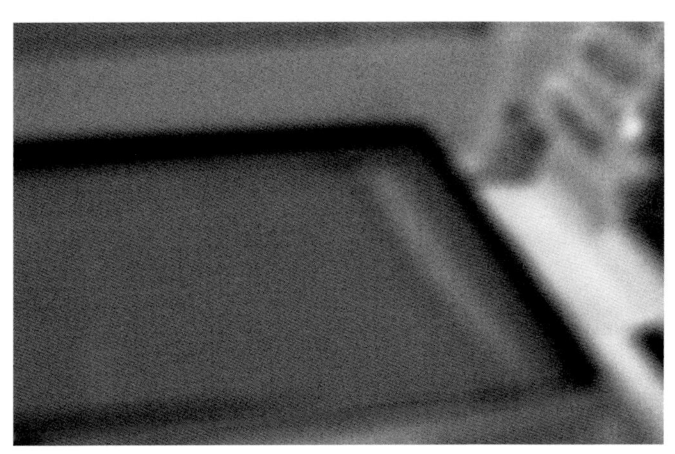

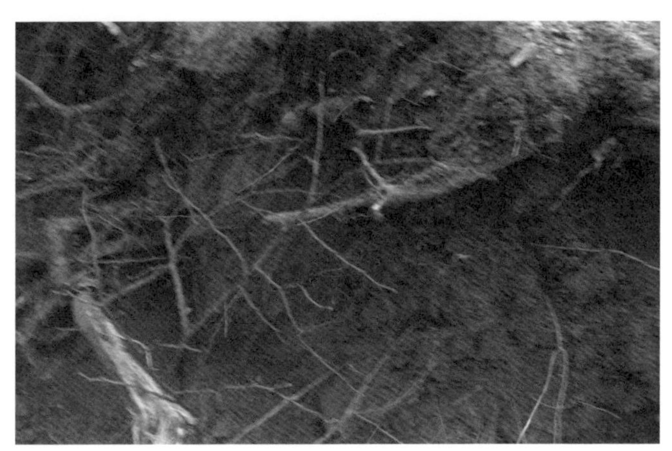

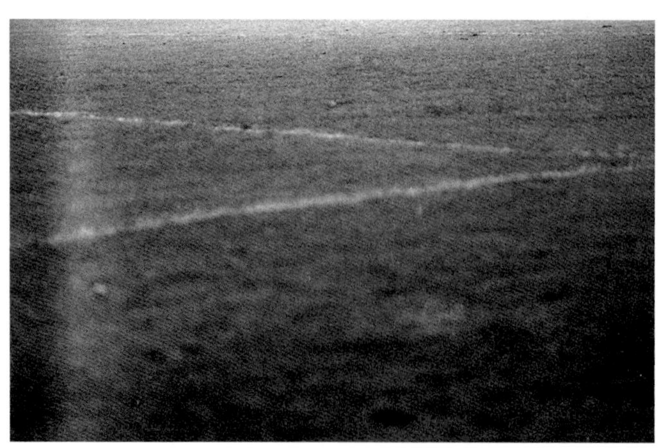

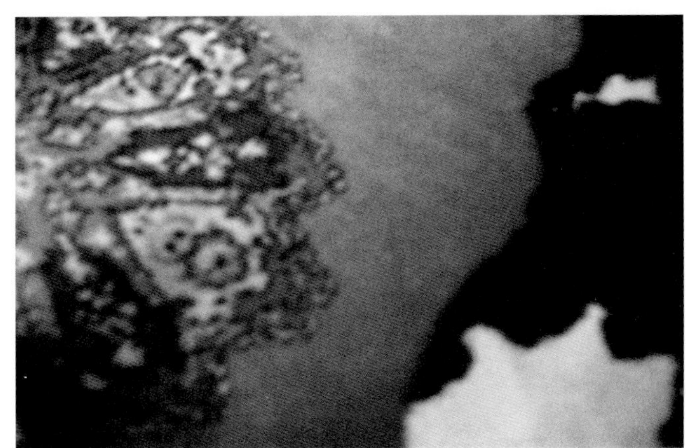

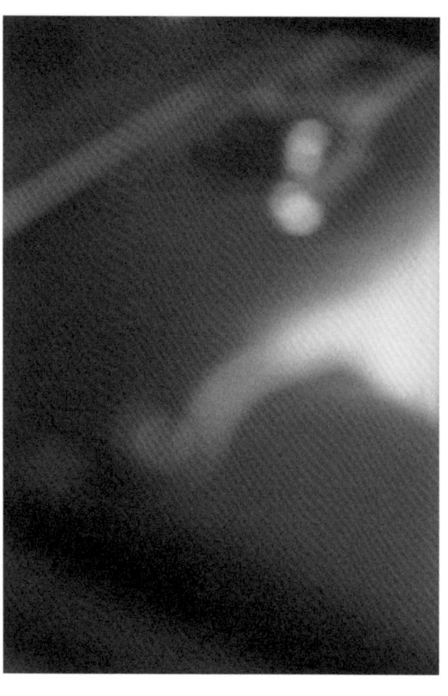

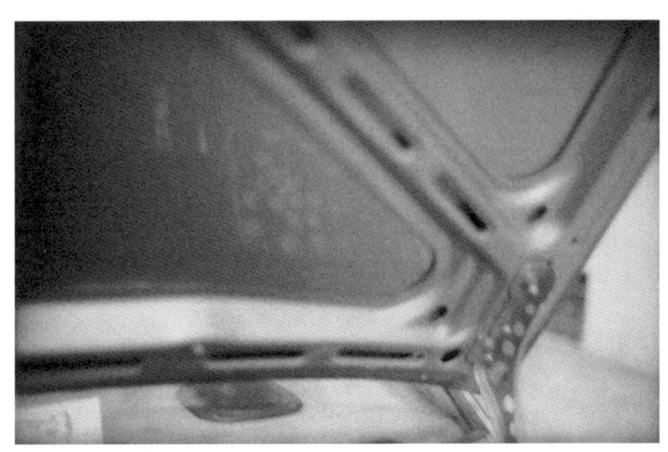

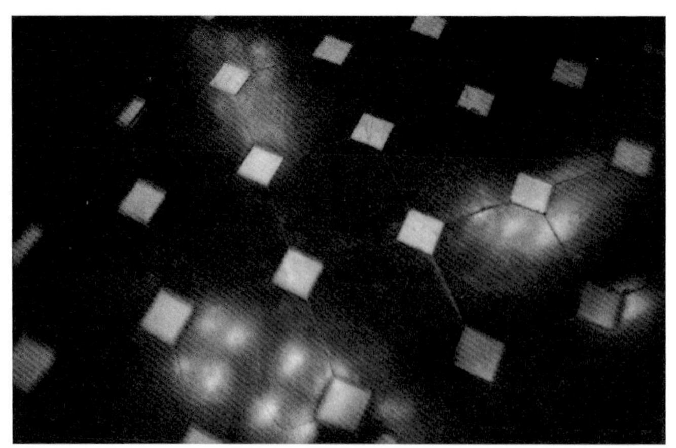

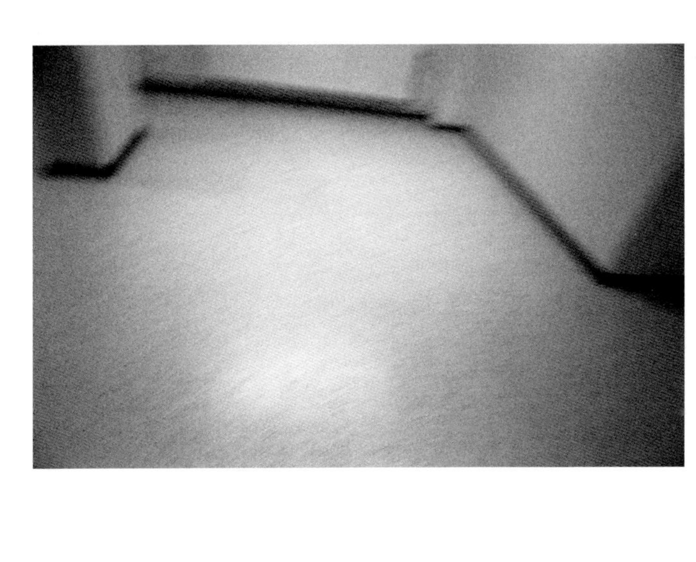

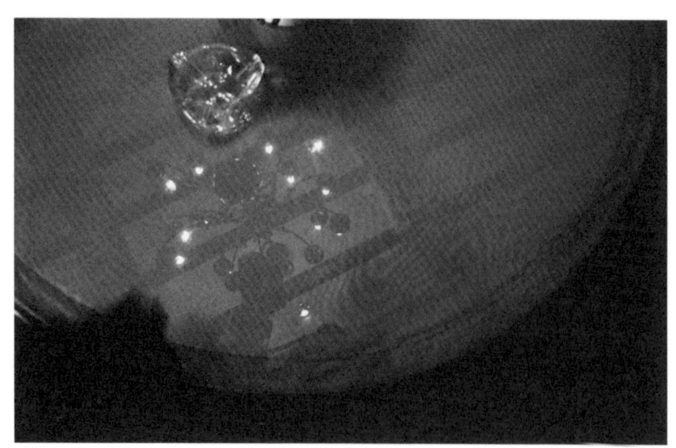

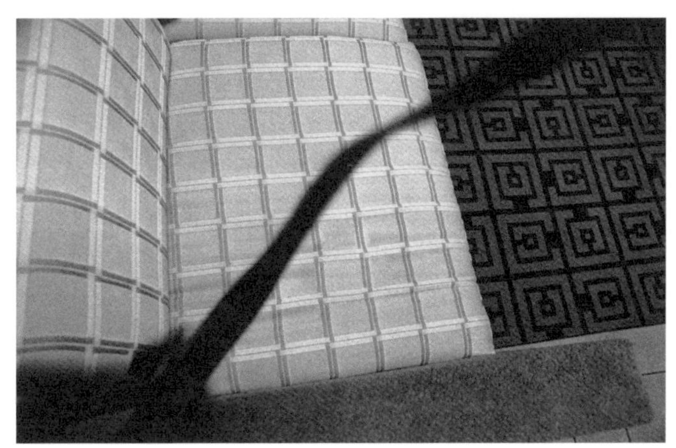

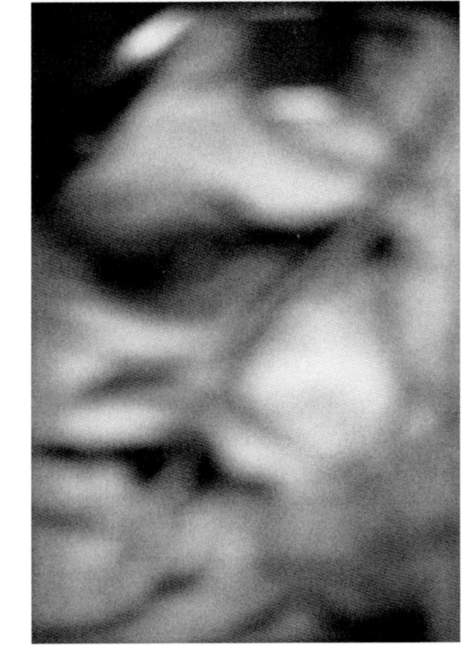

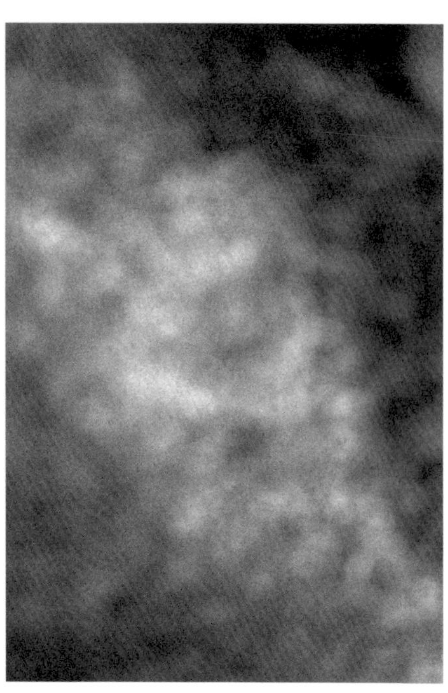

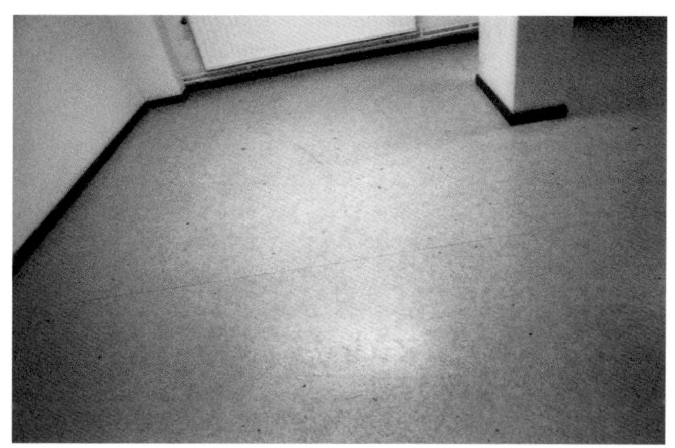

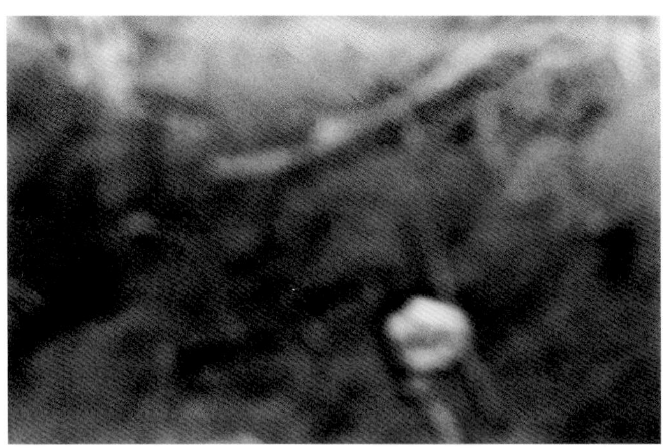

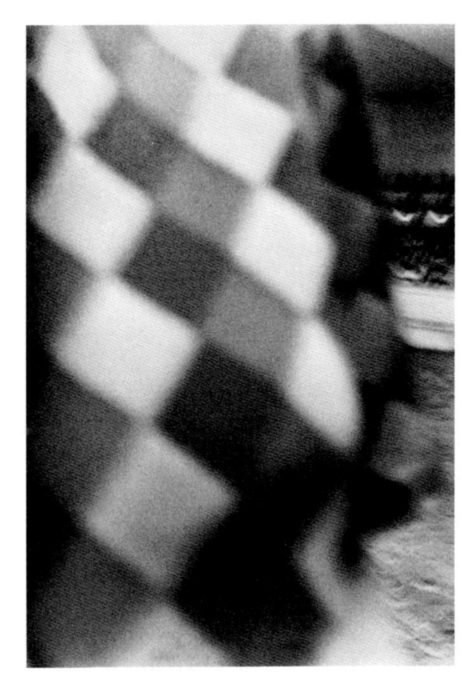

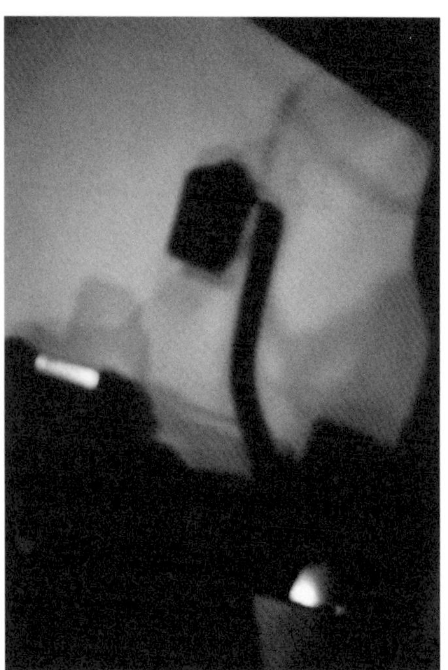

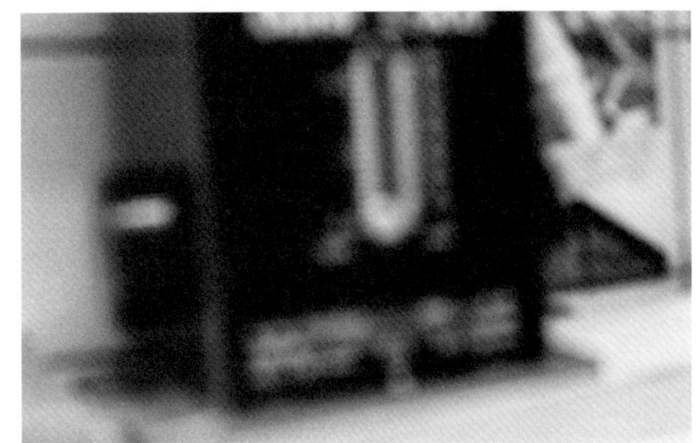

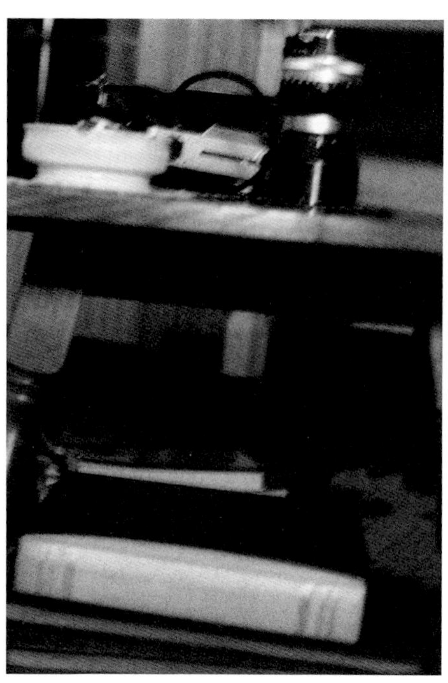

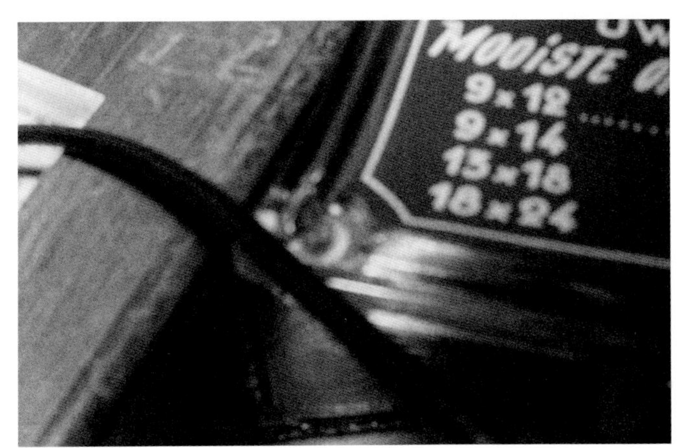
MOOISTE
9x12
9x14
13x18
18x24

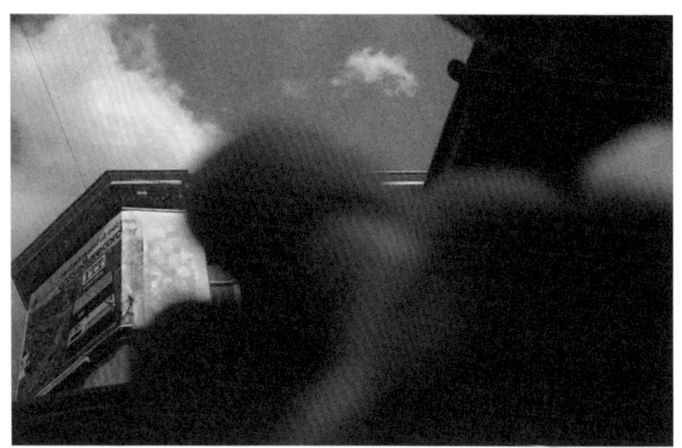

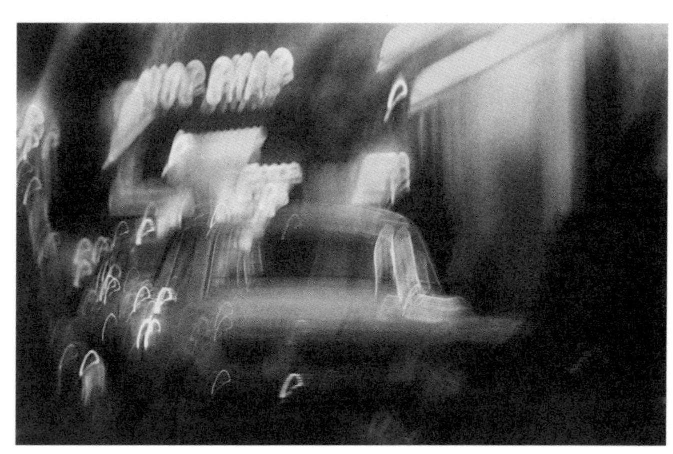

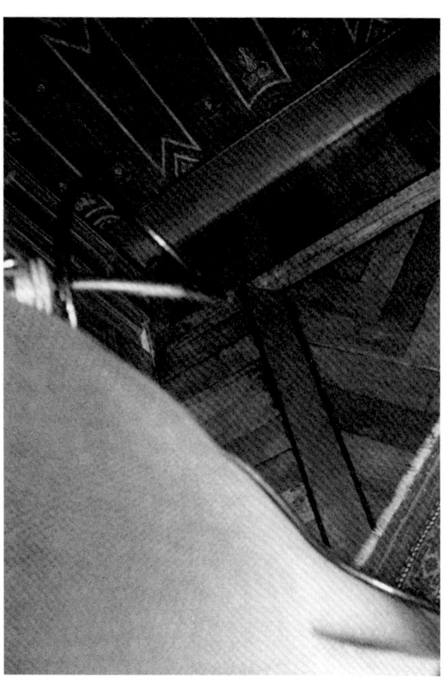

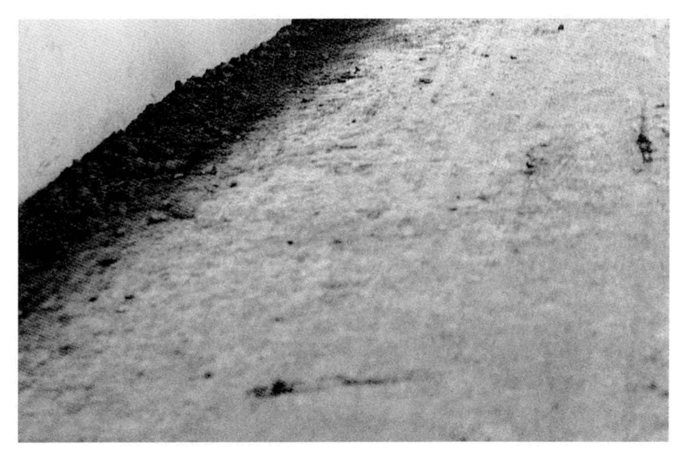

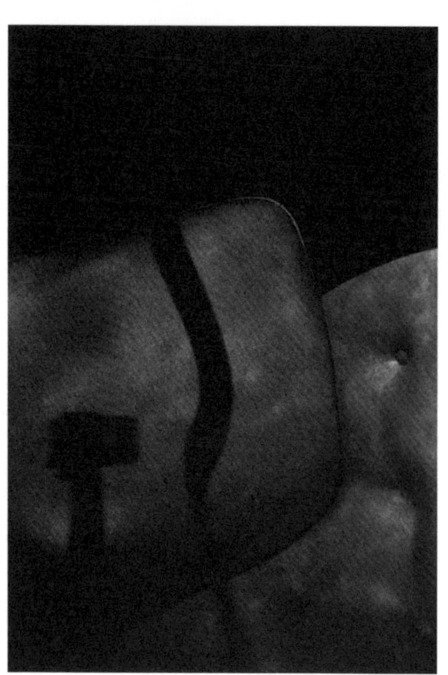

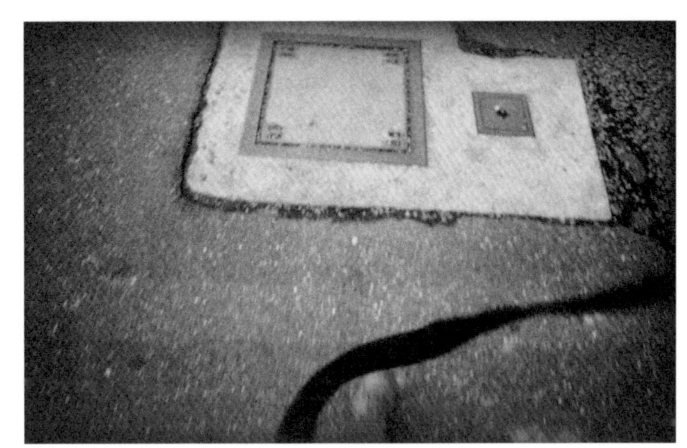

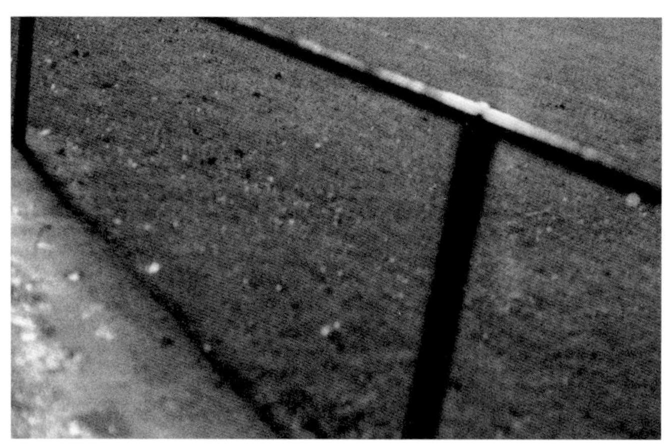

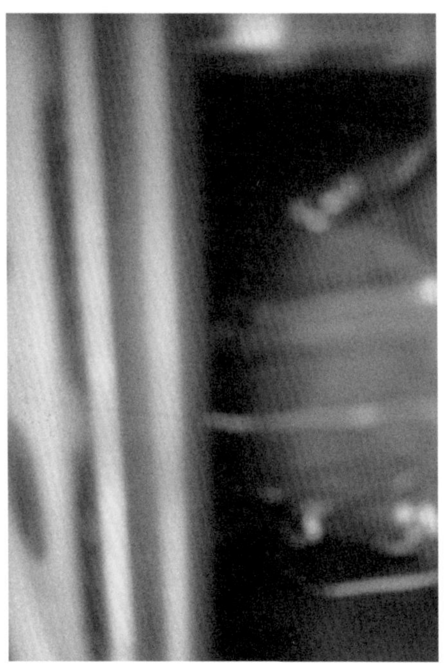

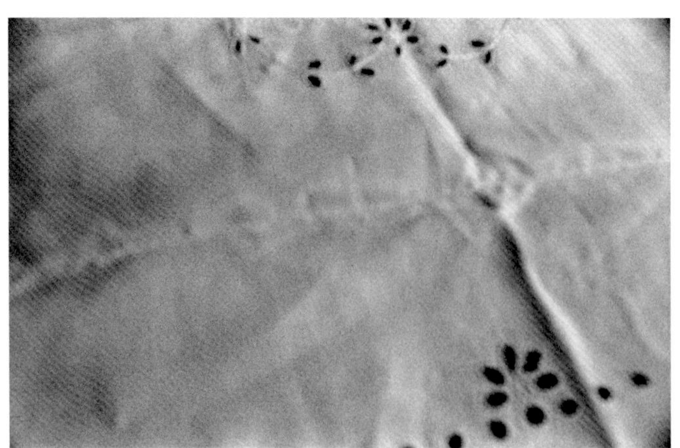

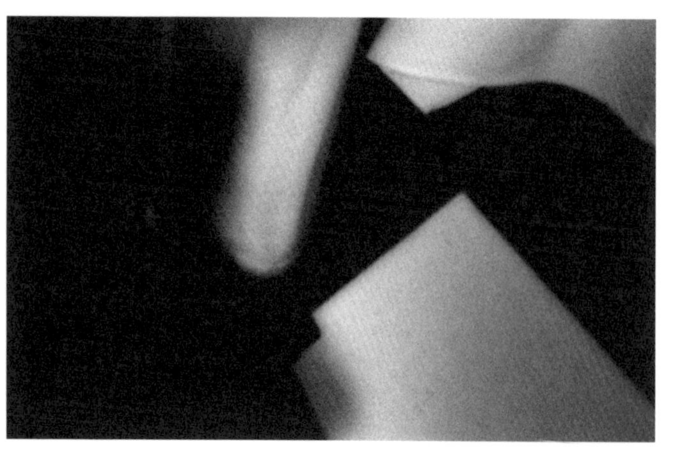

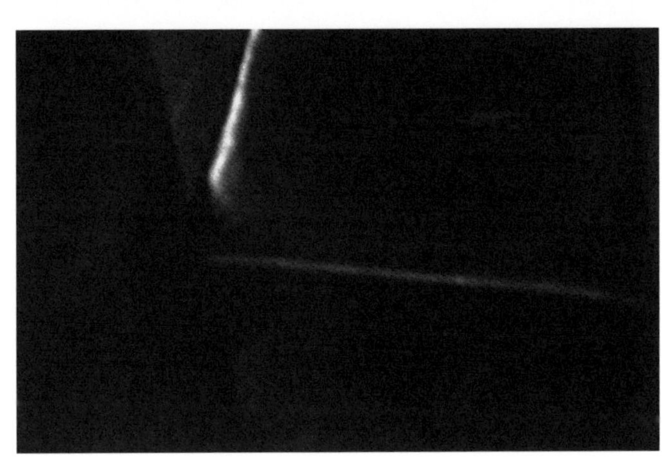

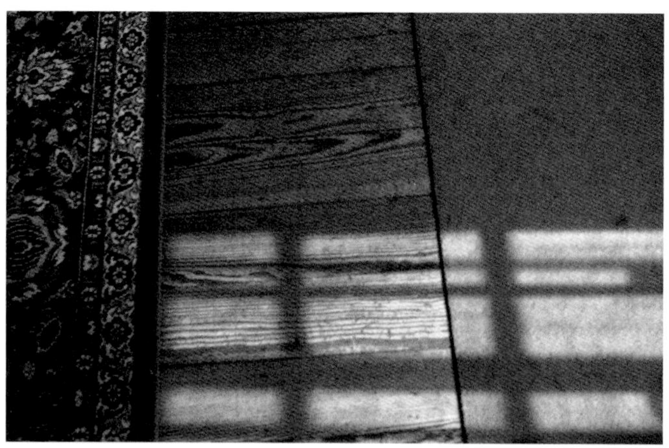

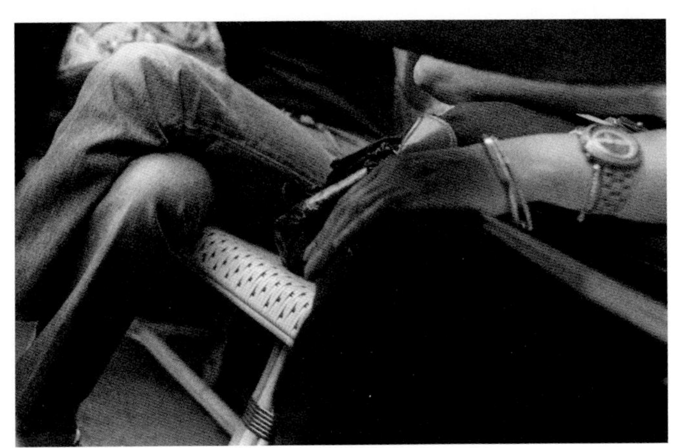

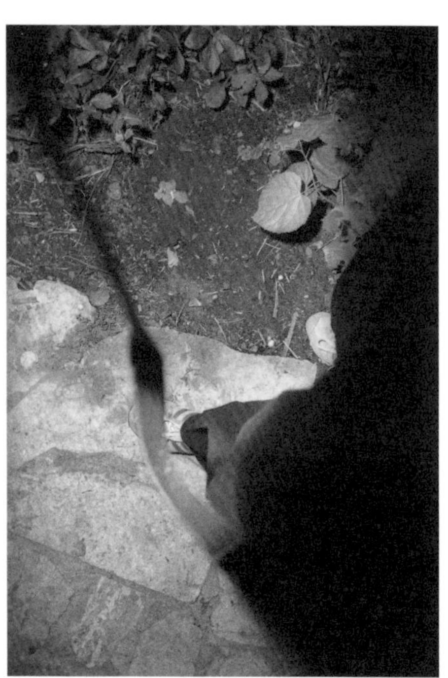

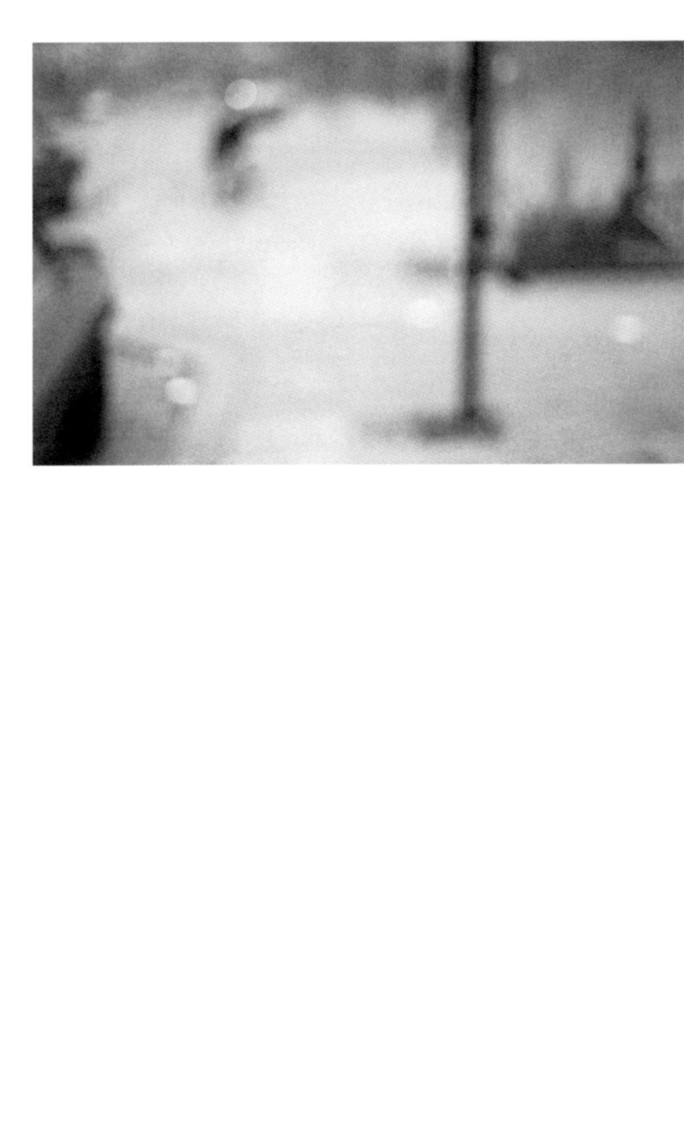

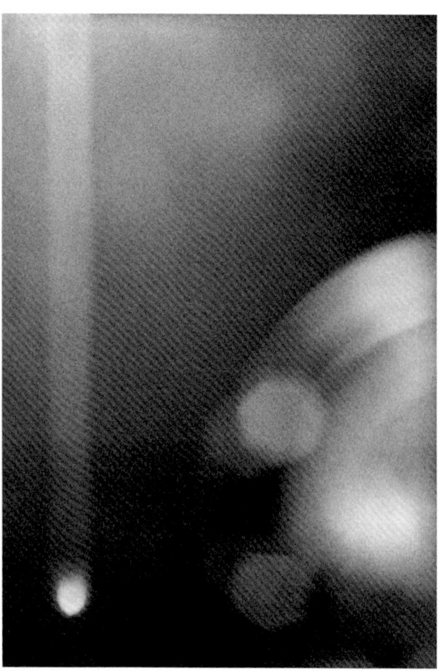

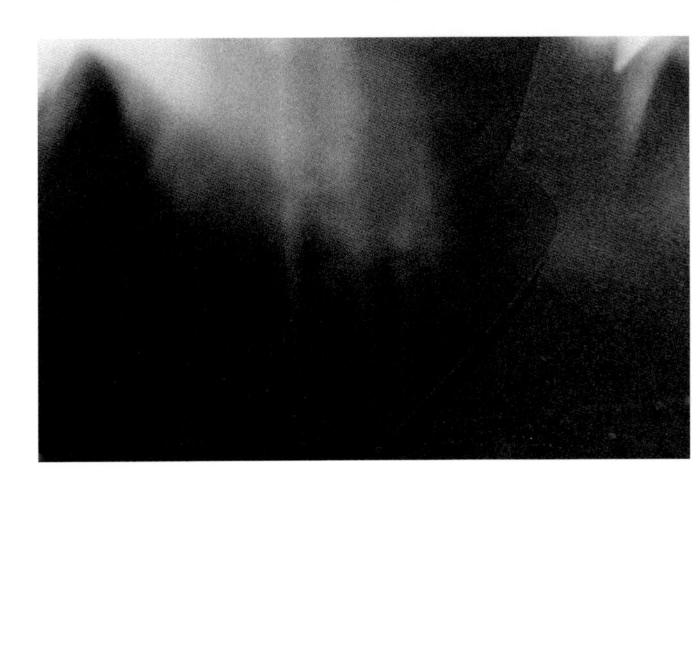

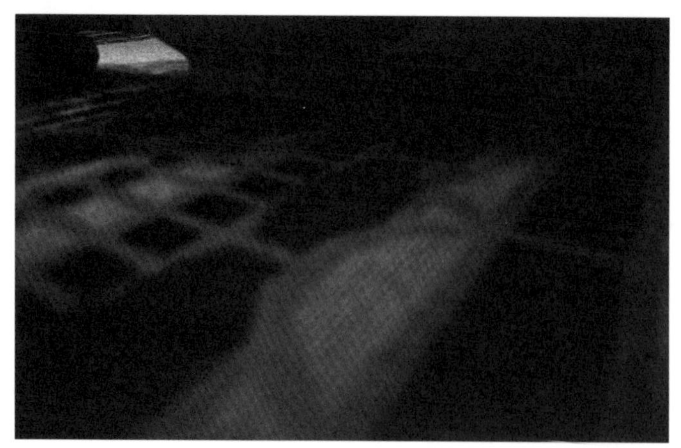

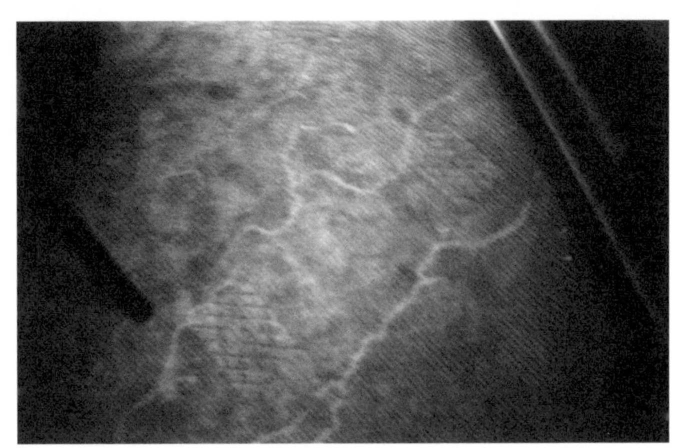

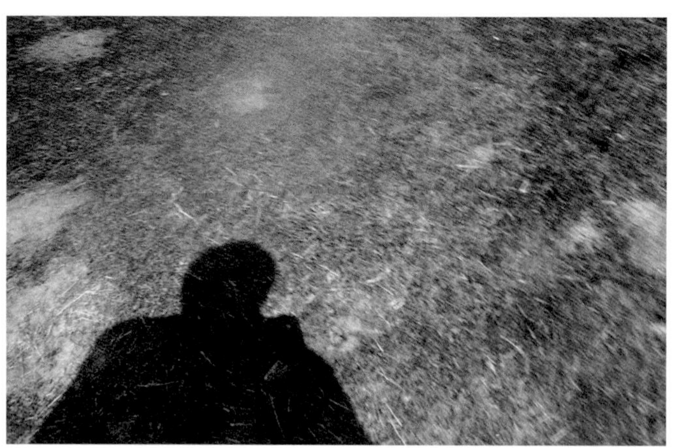

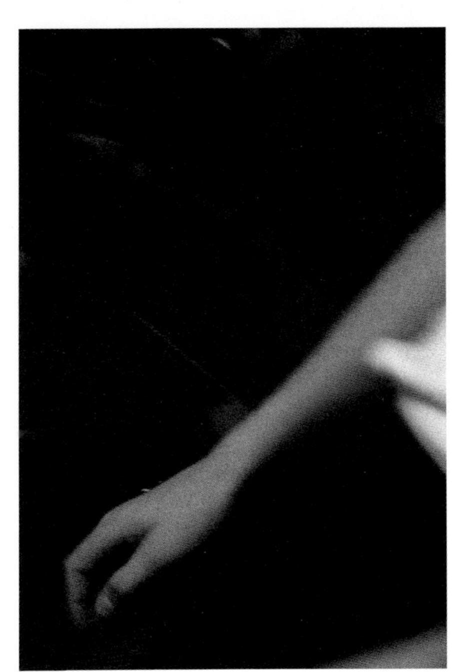

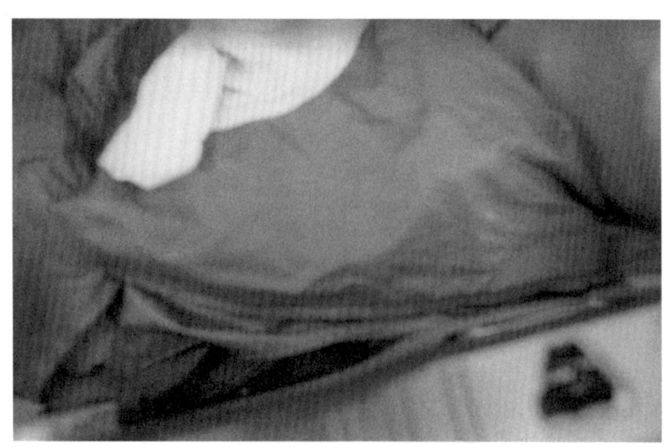

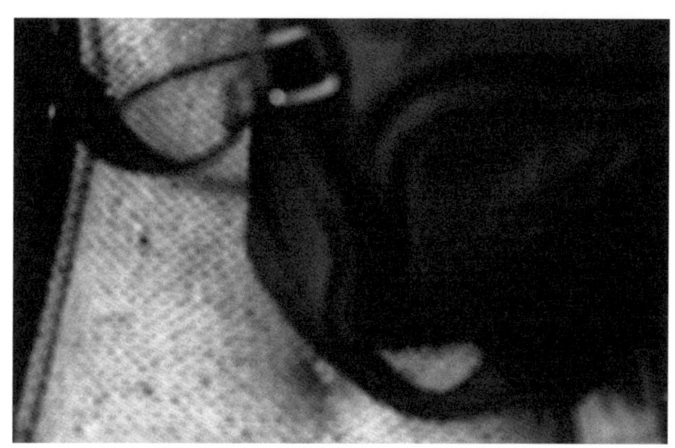

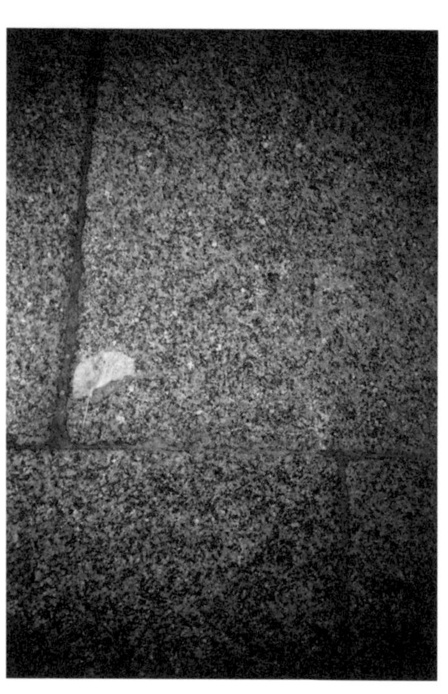

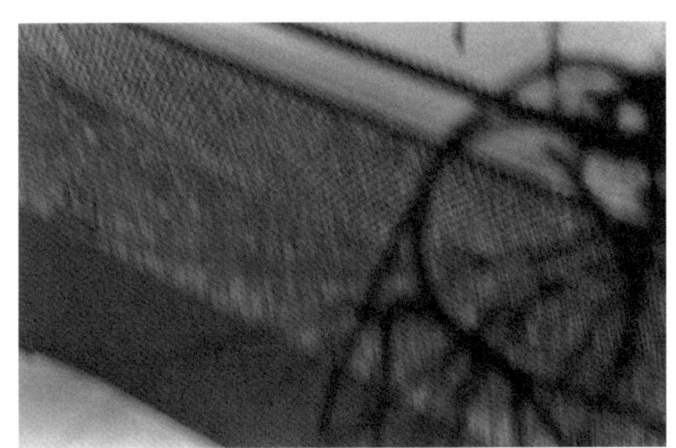

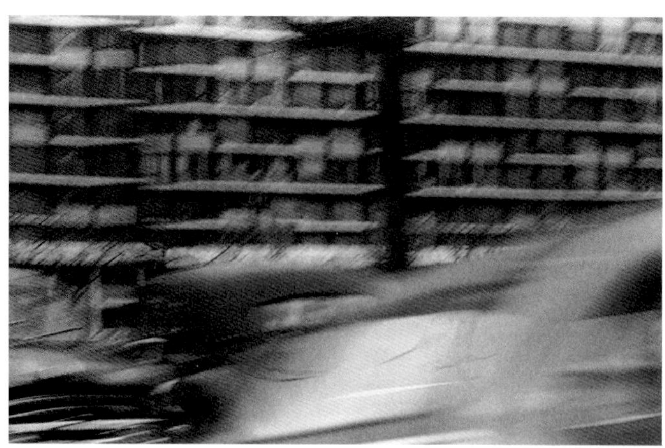

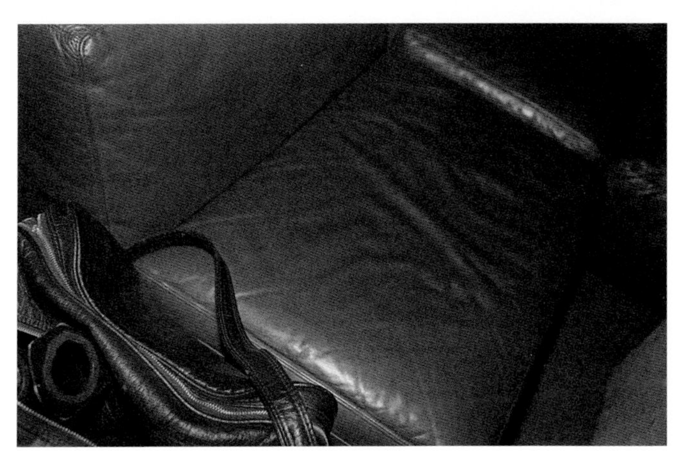

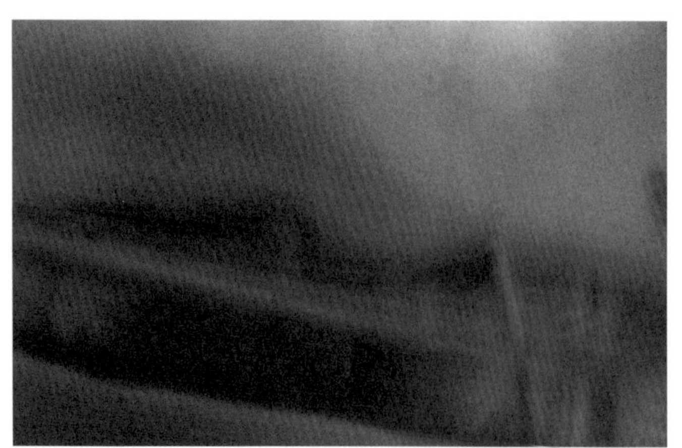

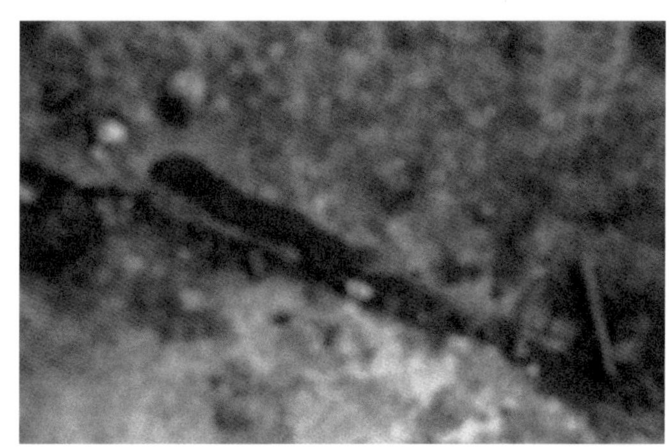

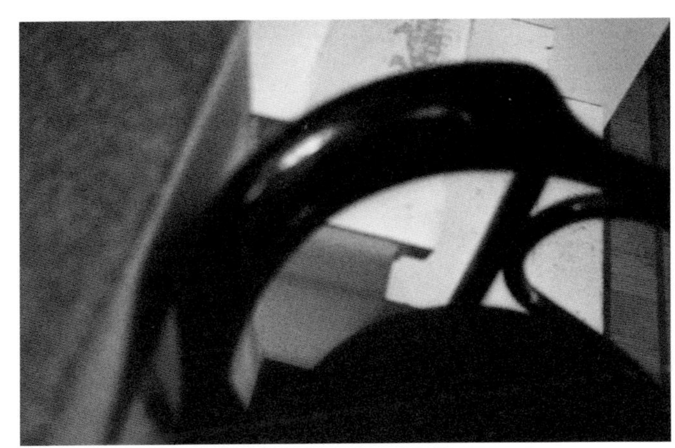

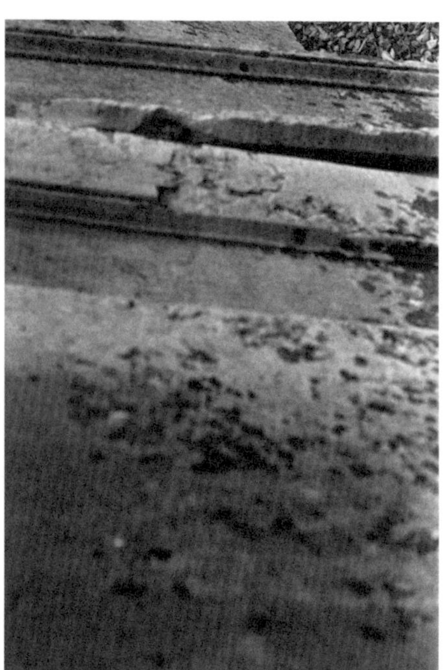

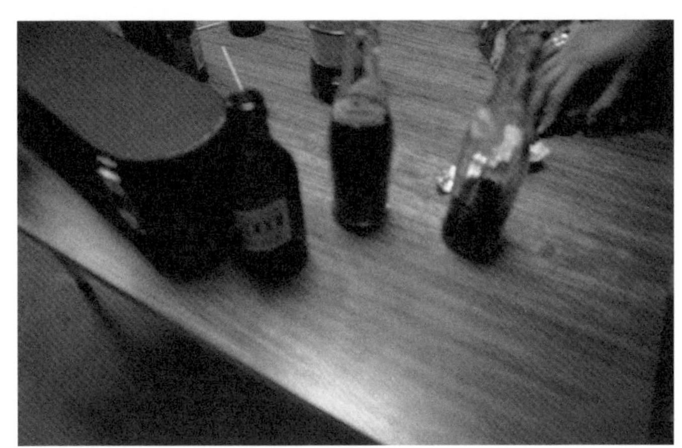

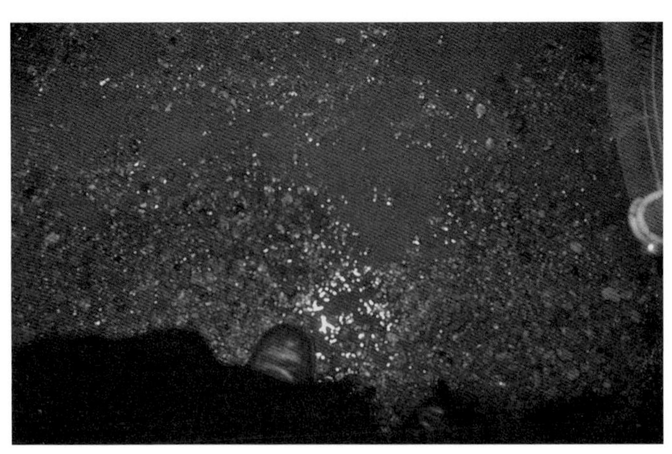

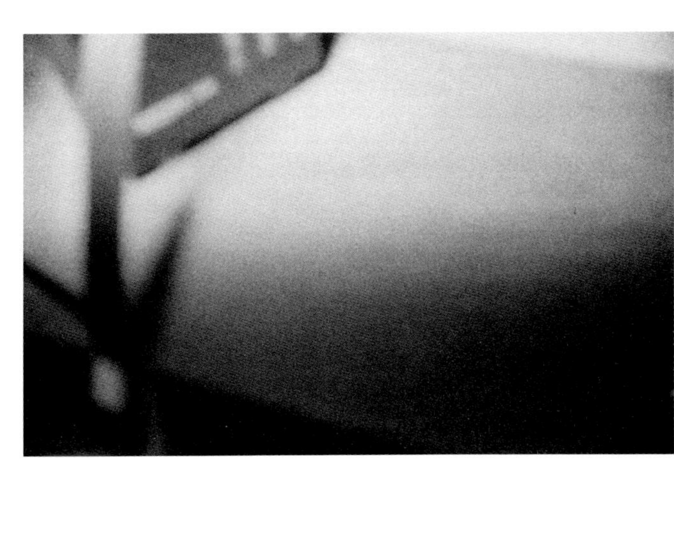

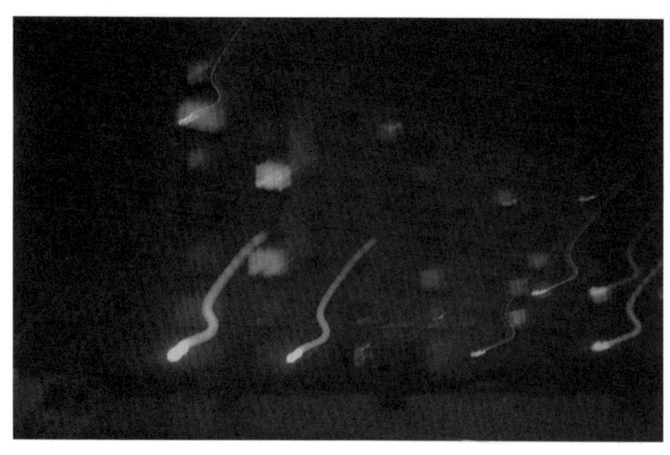

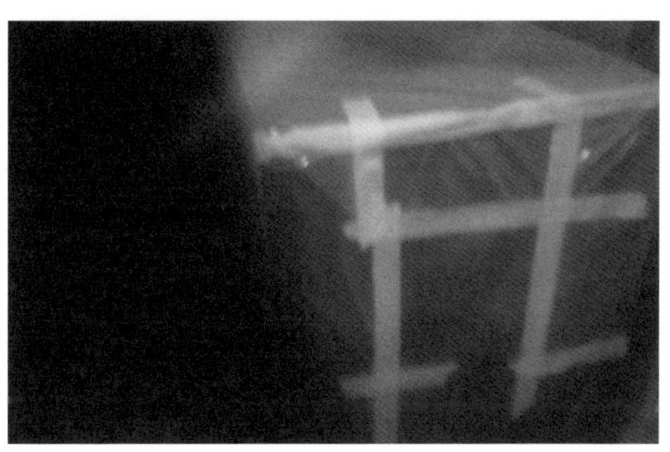

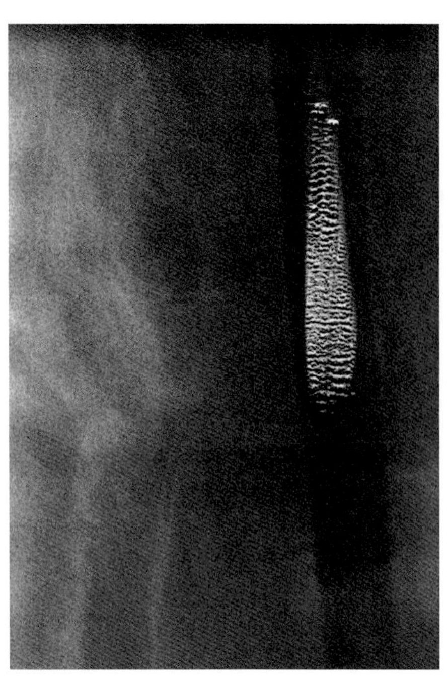

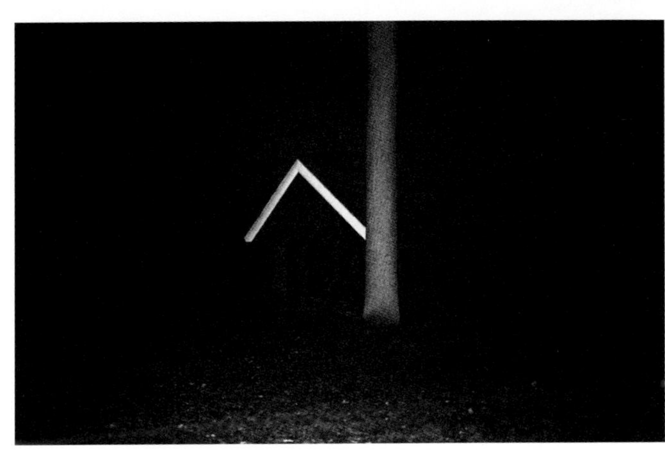

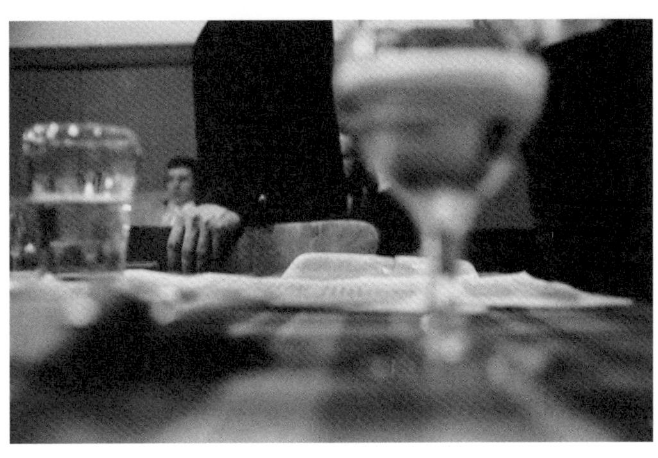

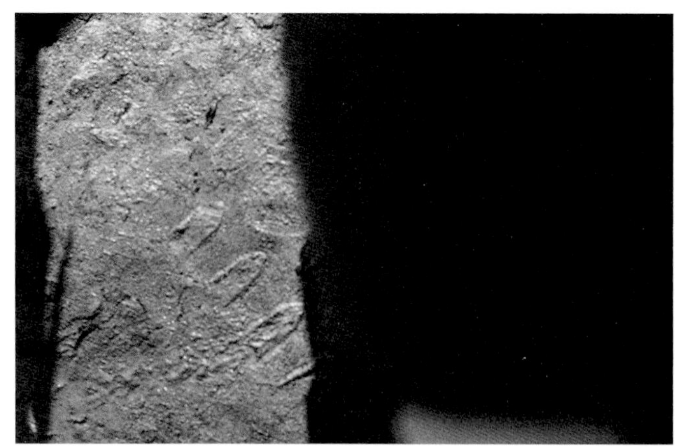

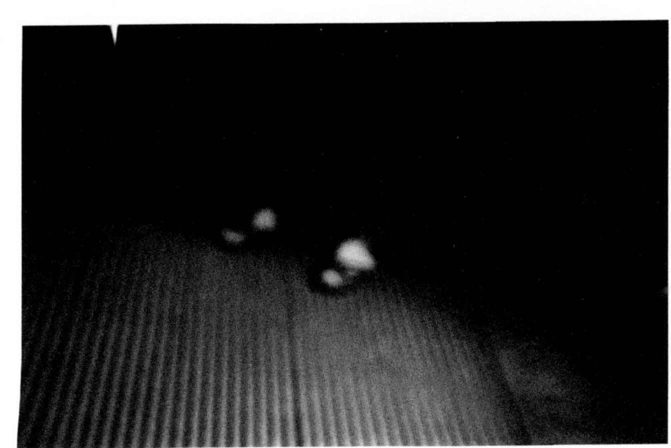

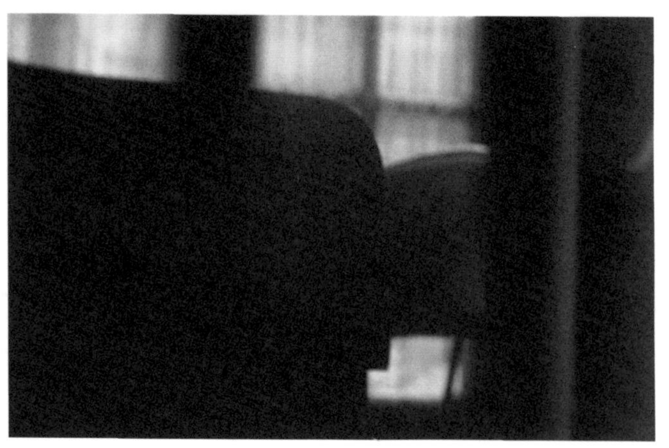

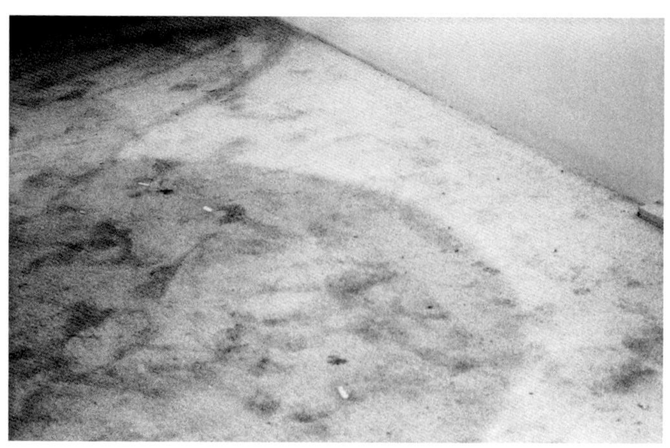

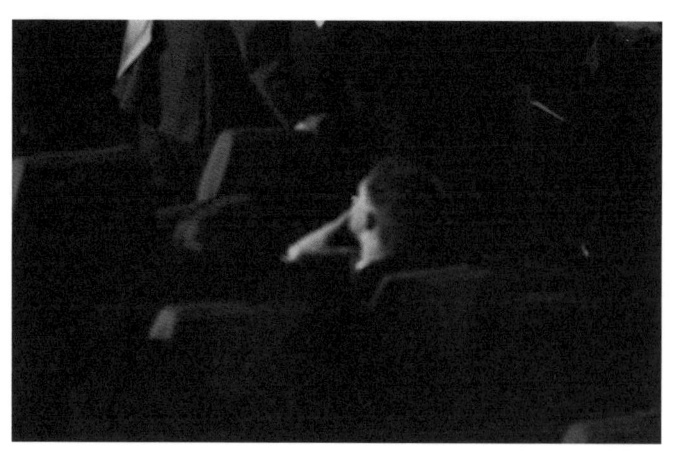

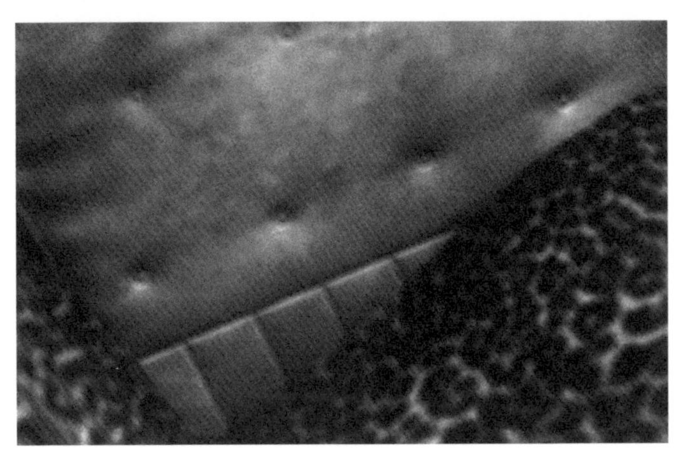

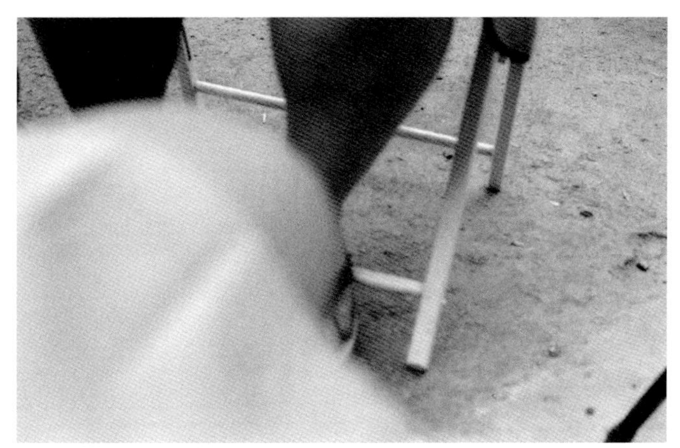

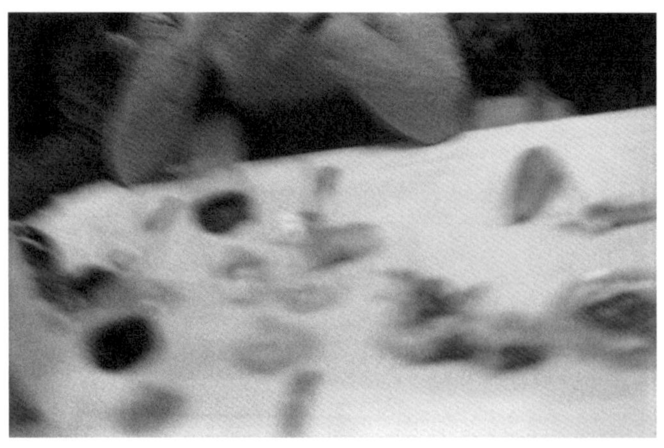

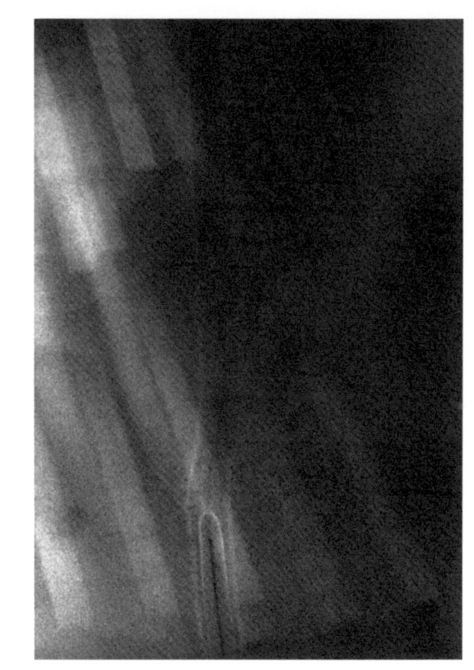

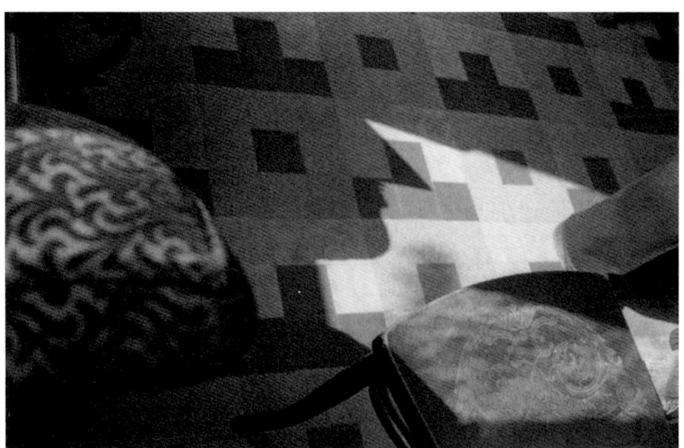

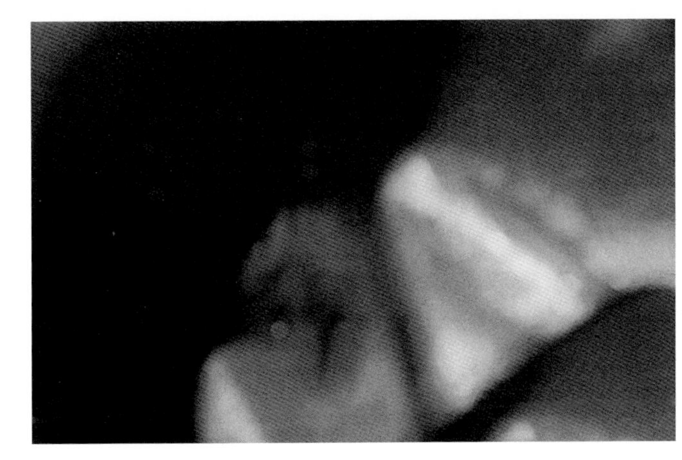

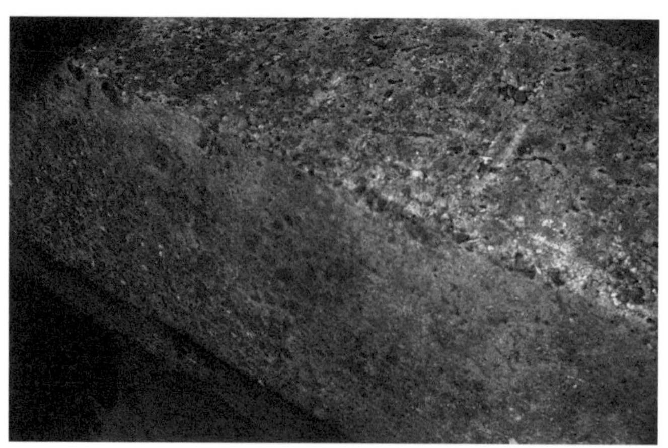

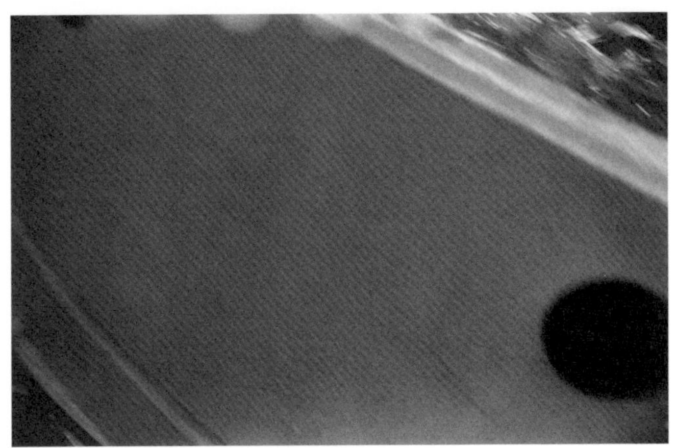

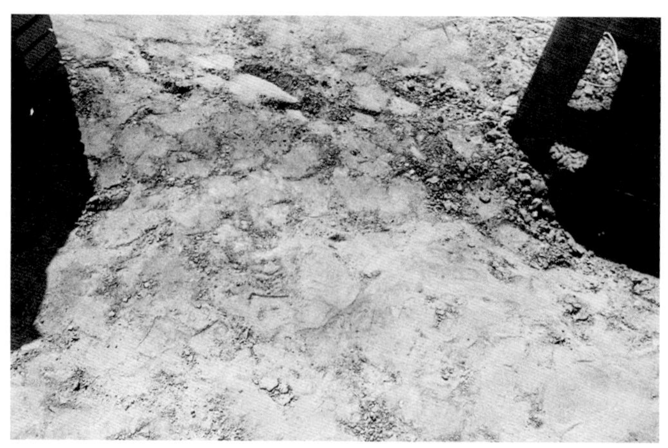

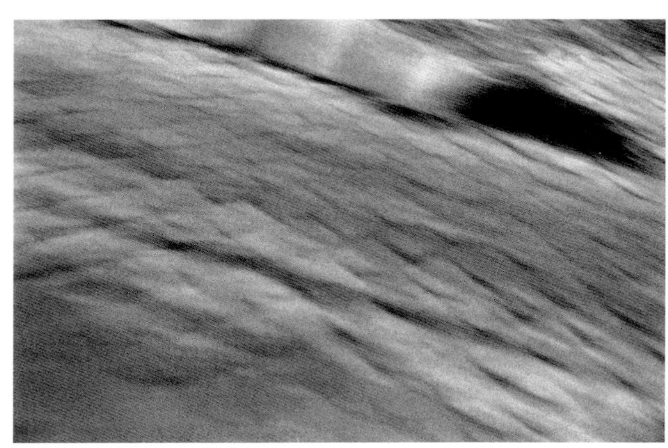

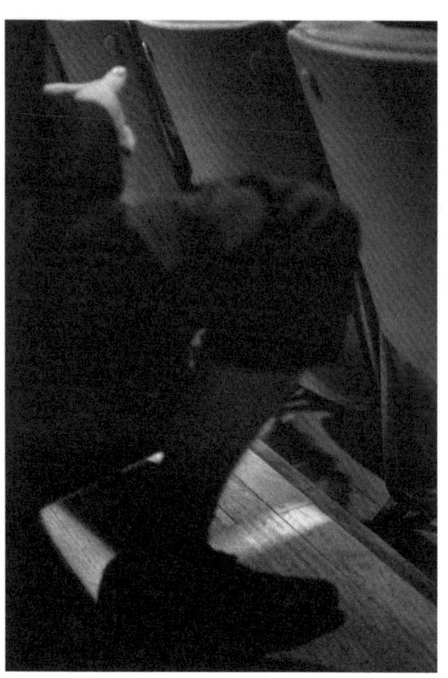

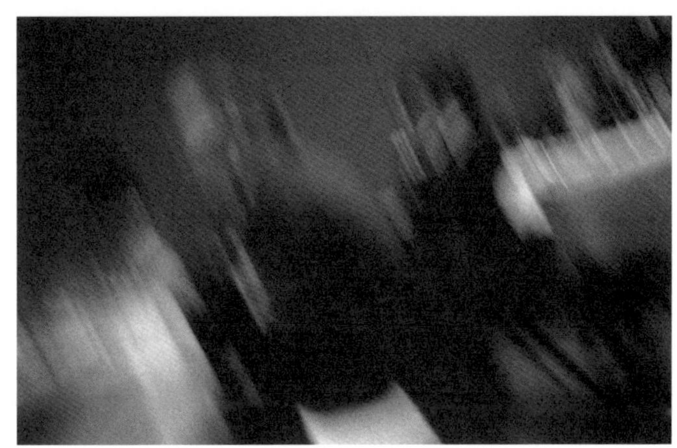

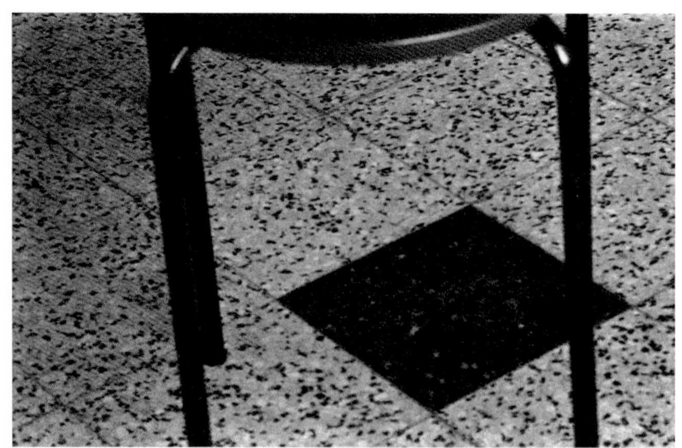

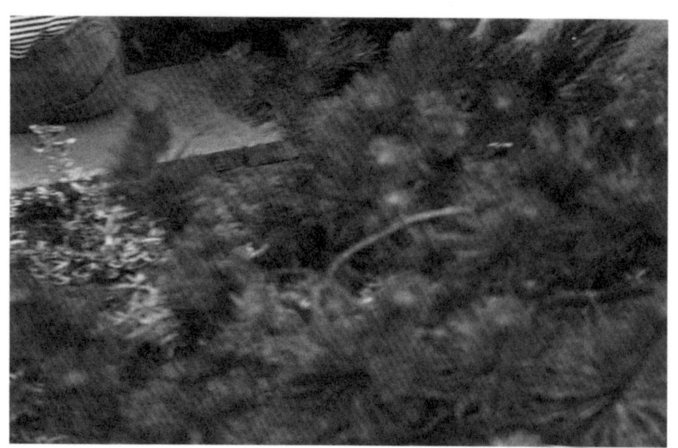

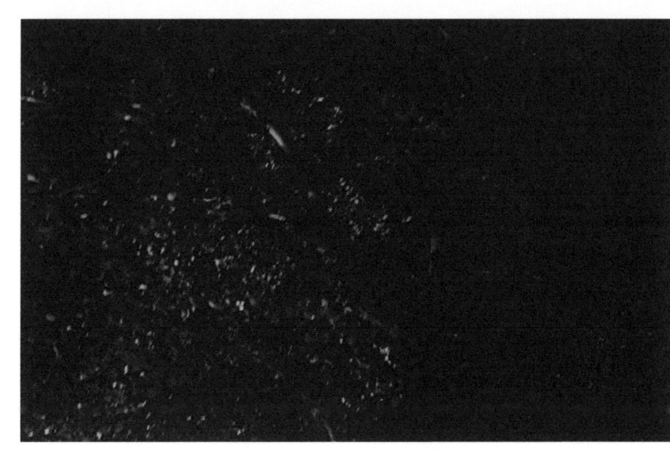

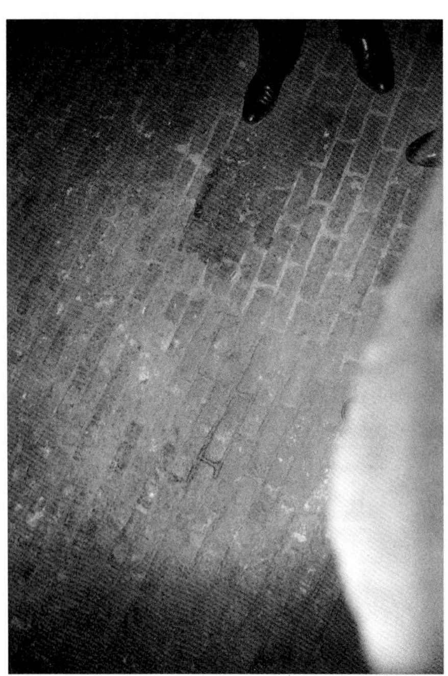

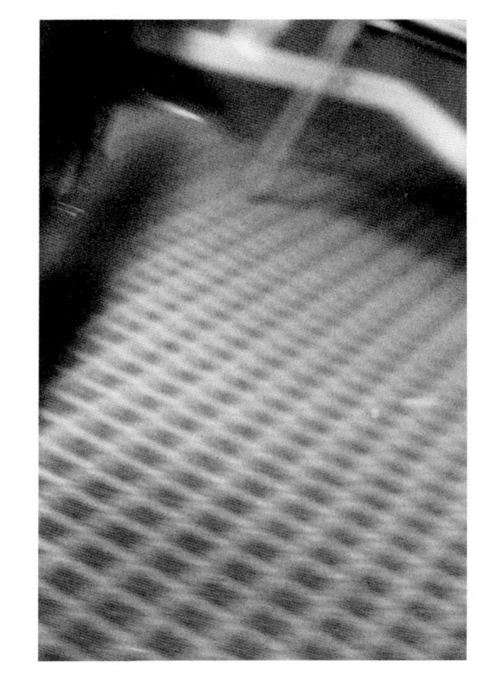

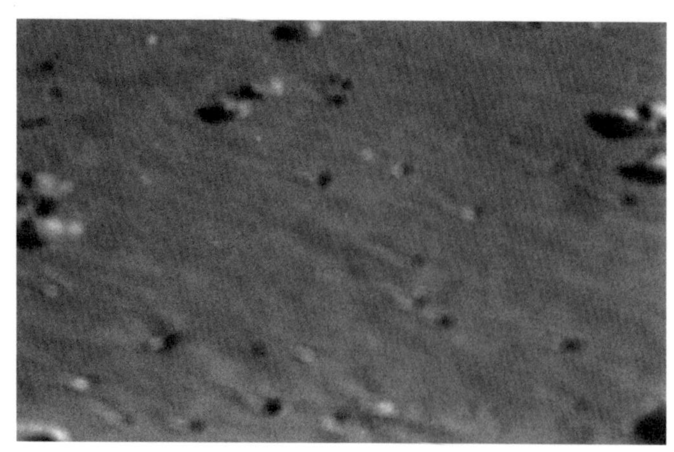

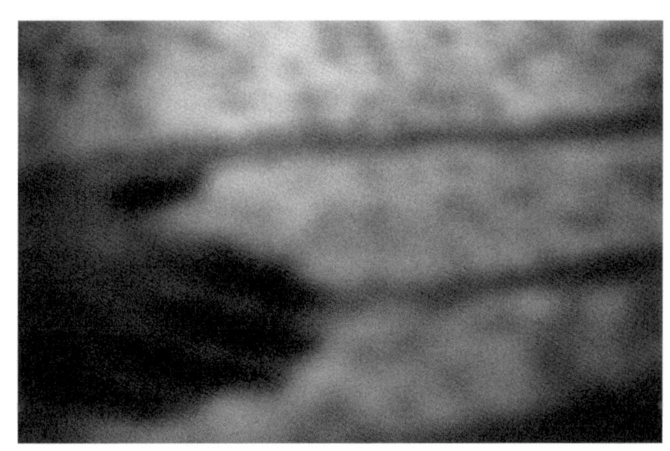

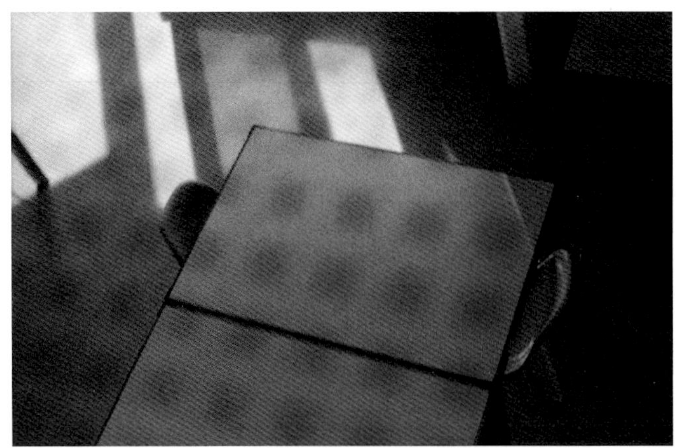

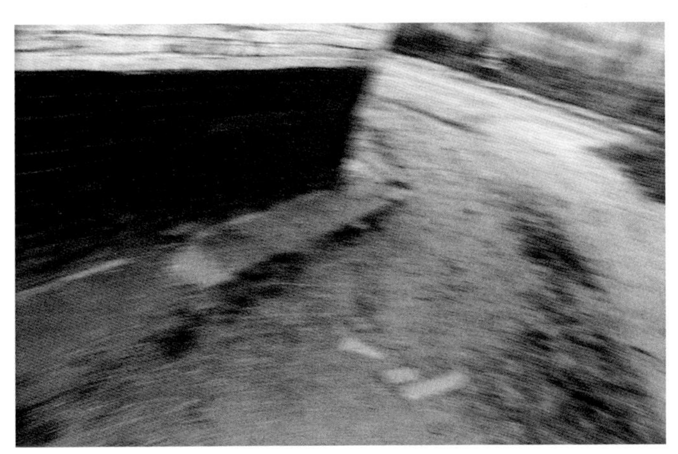

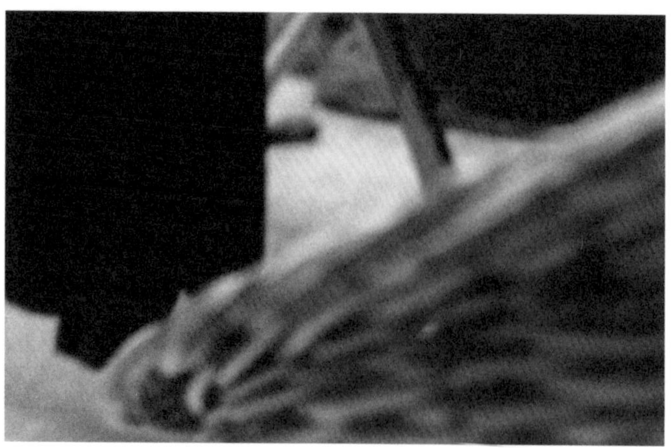

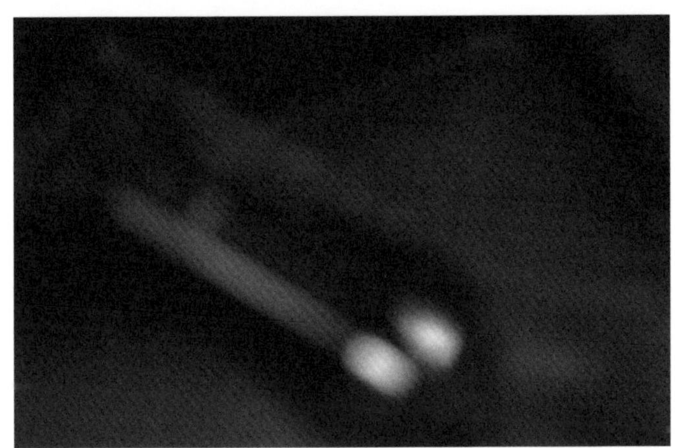

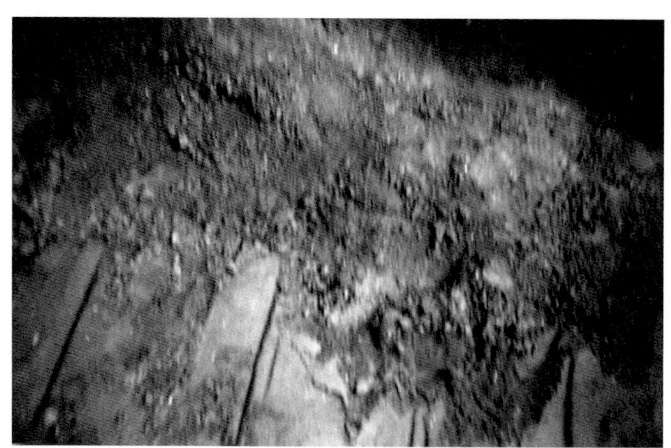

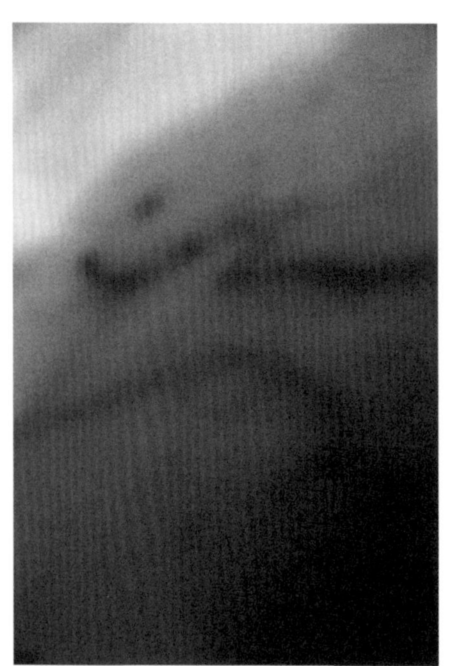

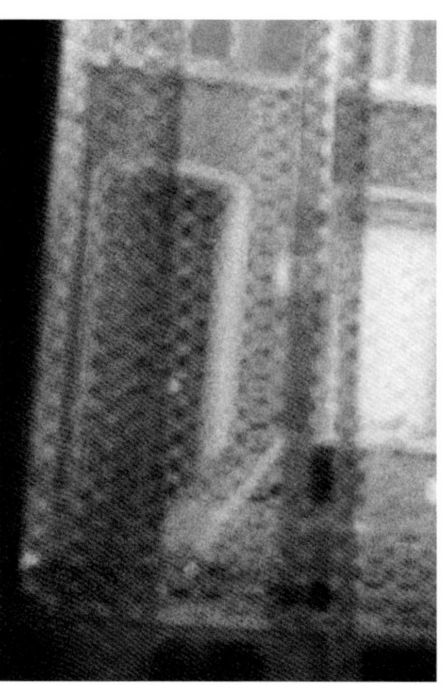

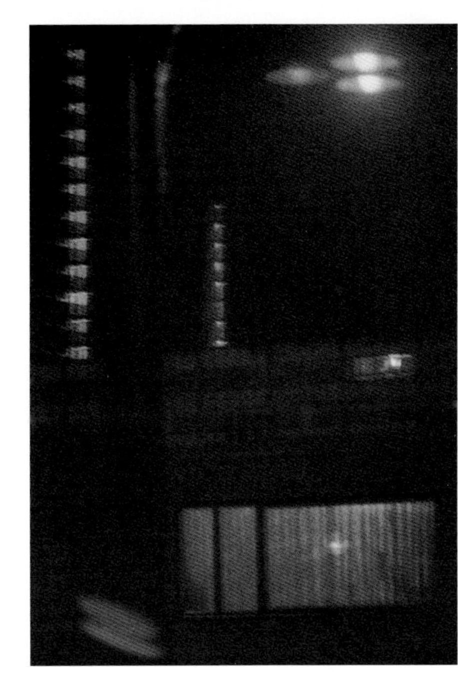

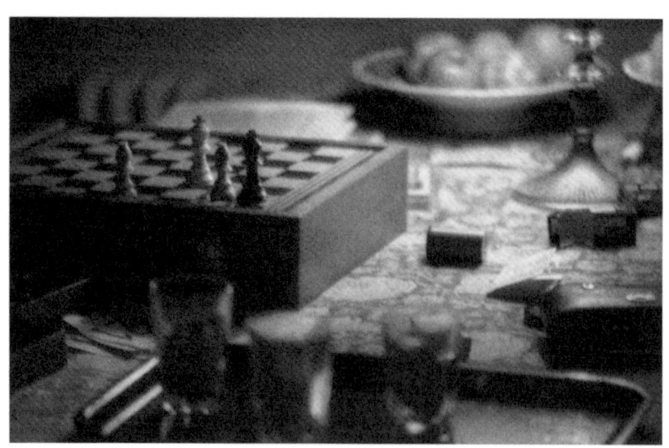

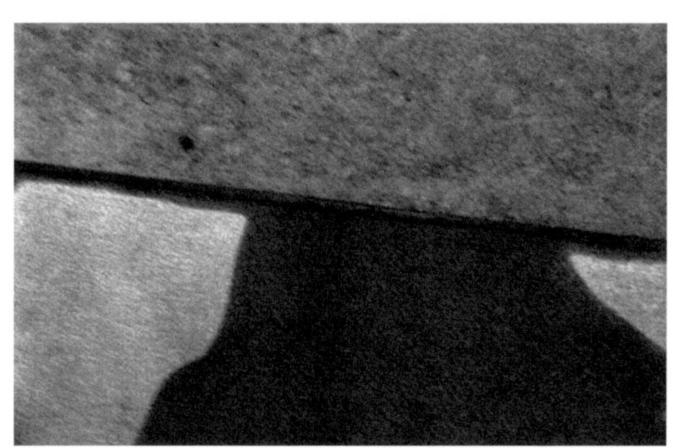

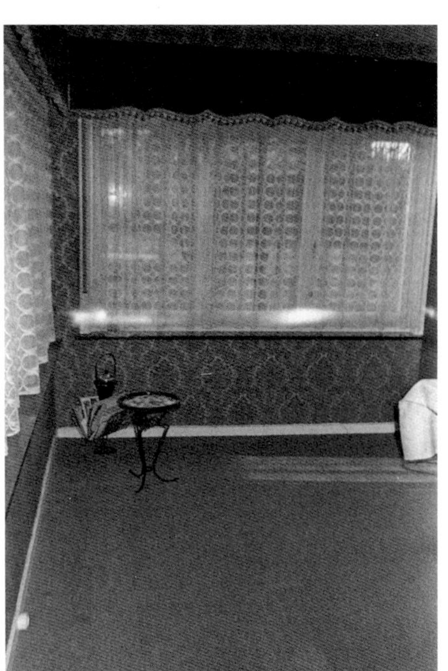

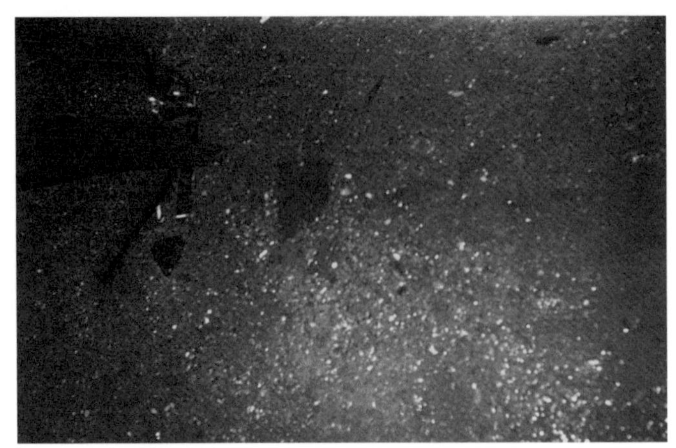

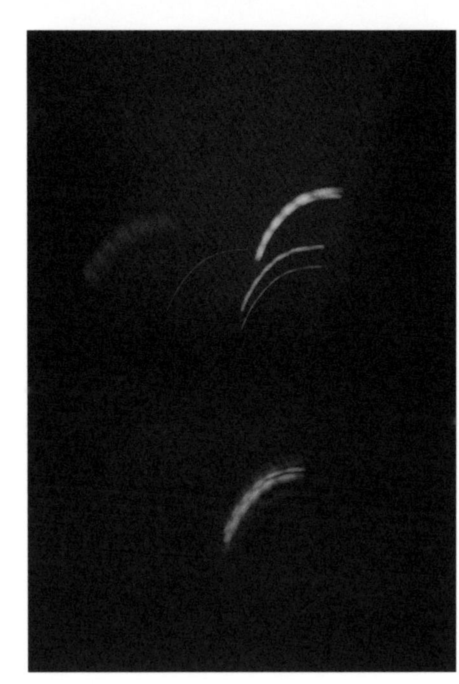

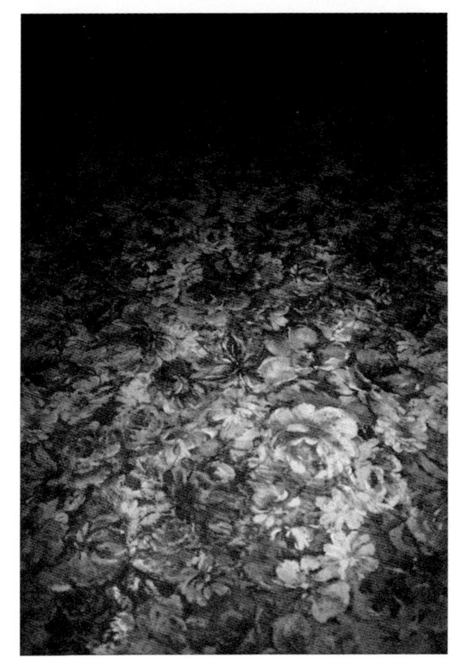

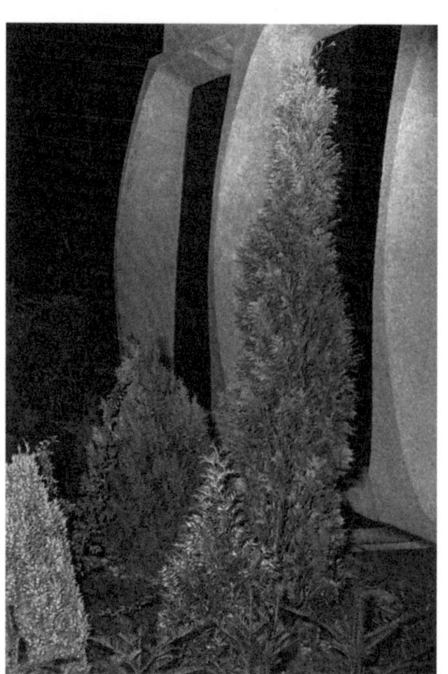

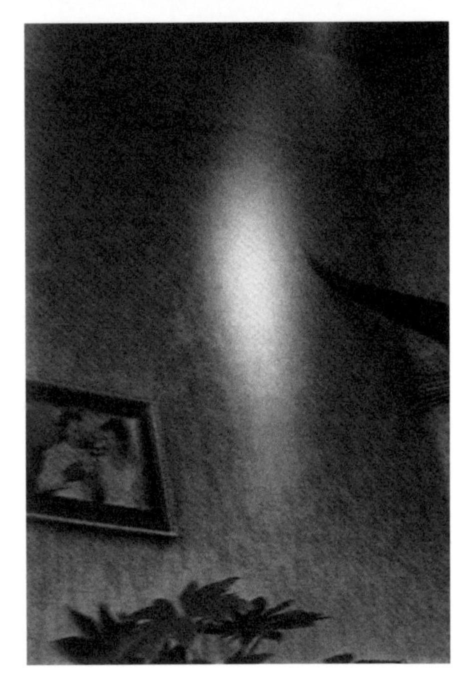

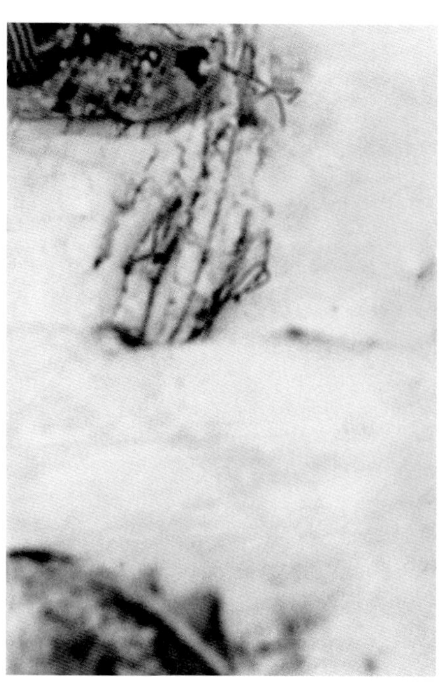

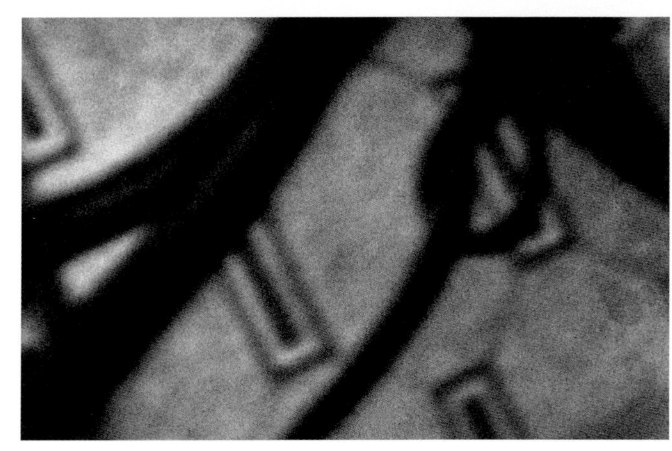

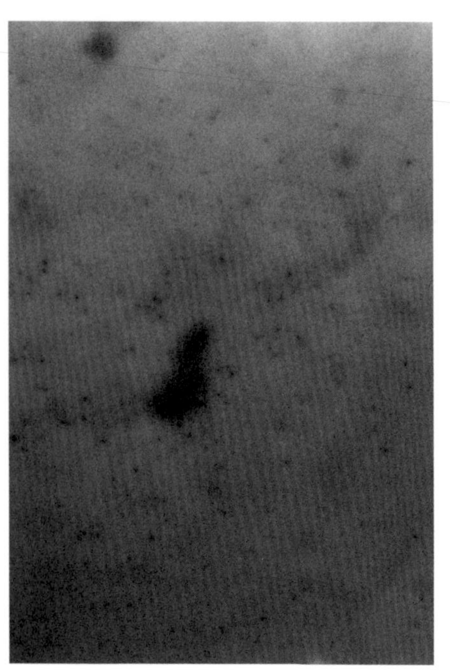

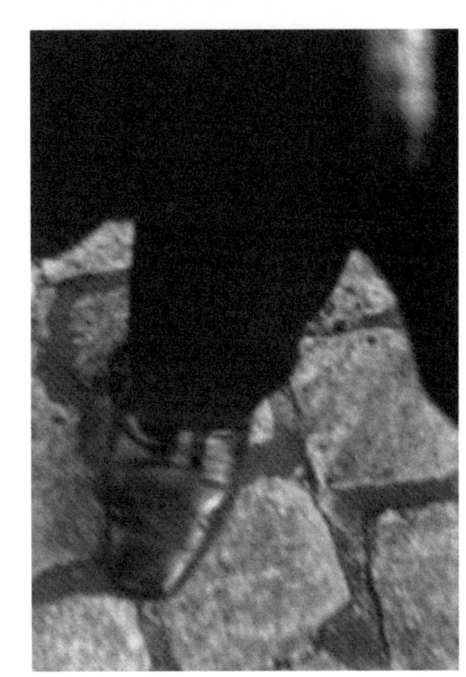

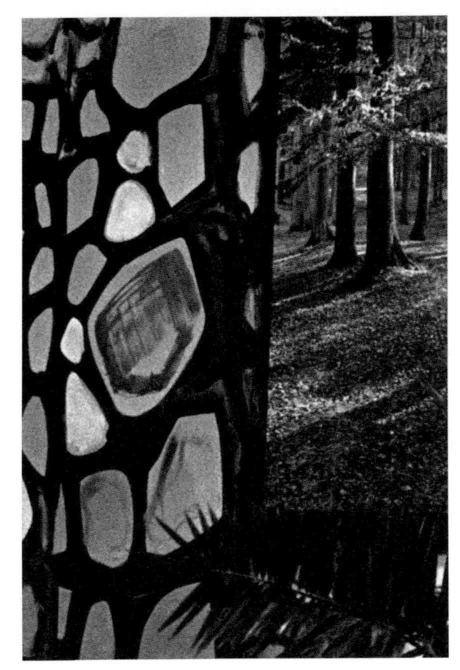

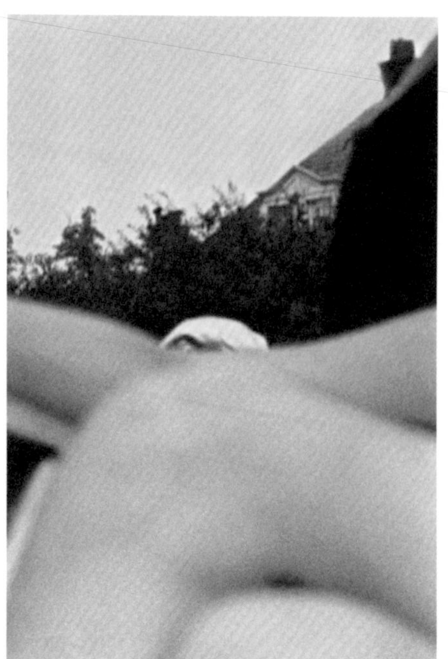

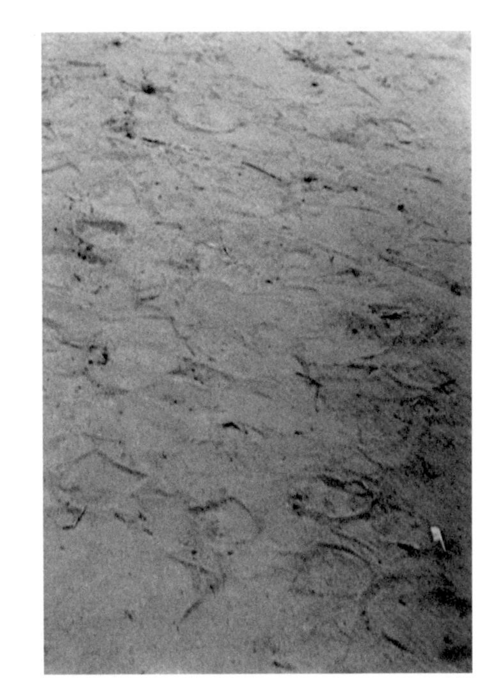

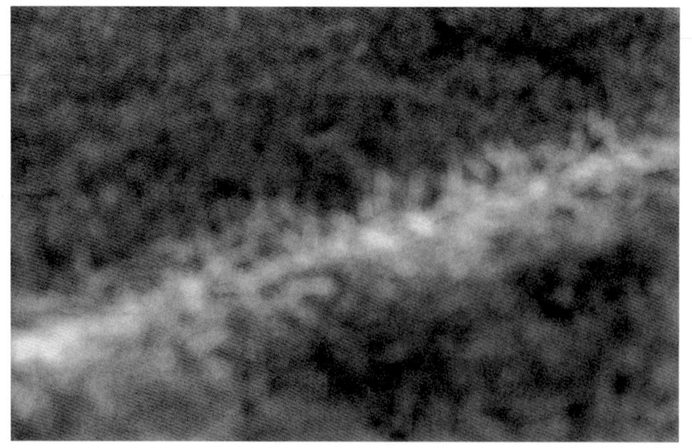

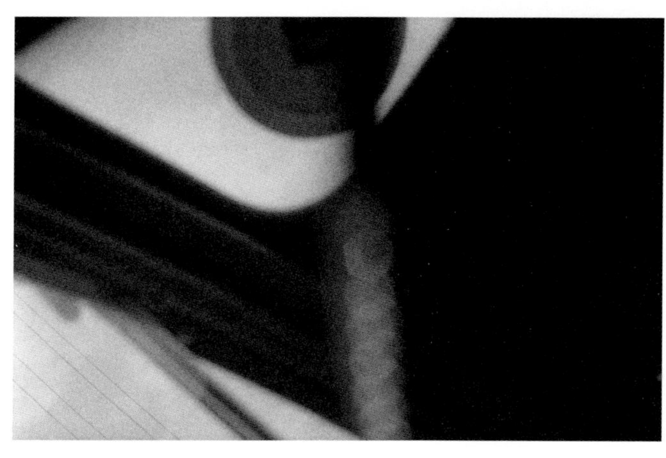

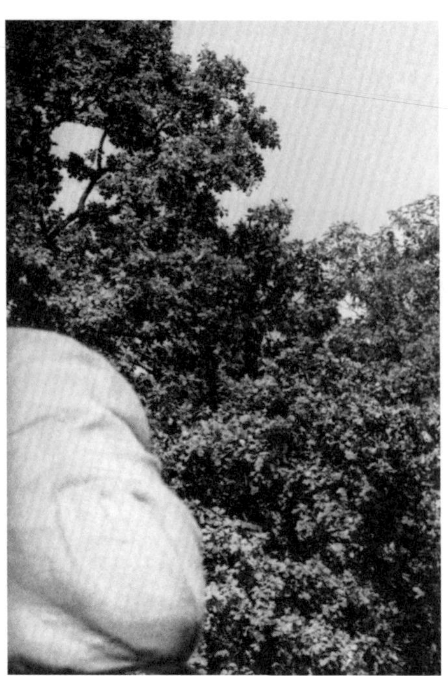

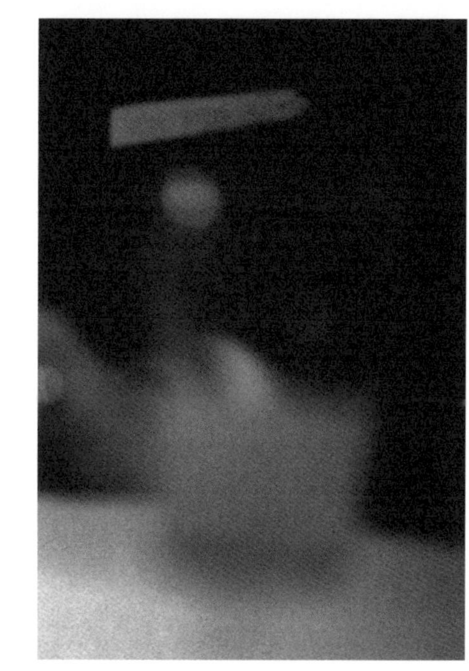

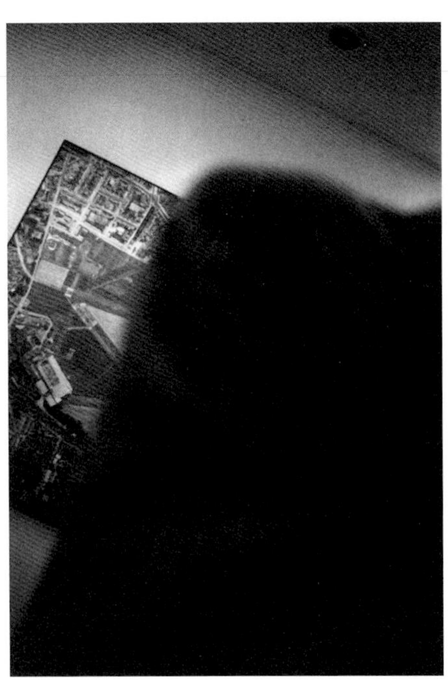

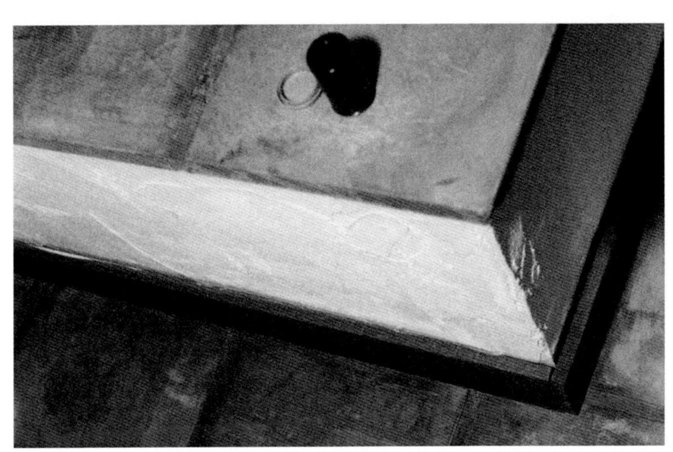

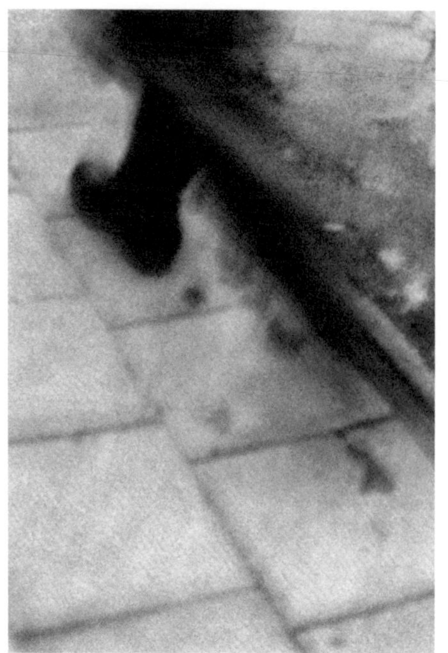

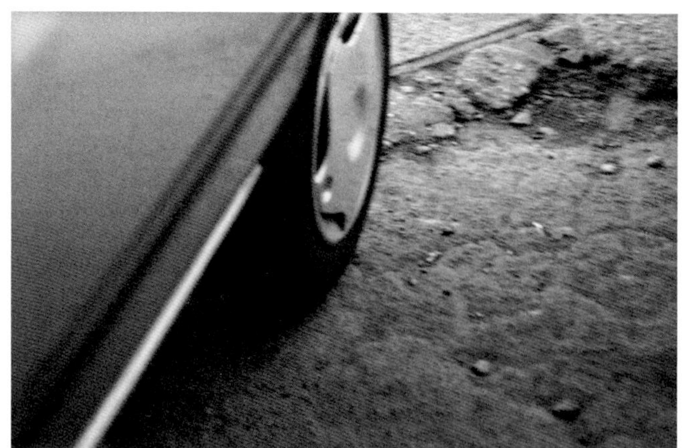

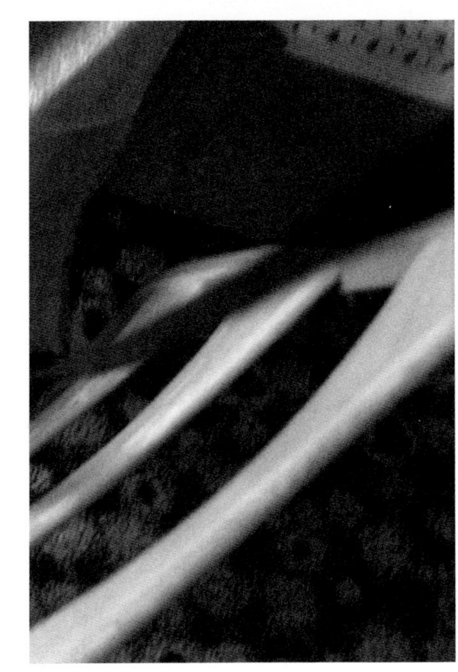

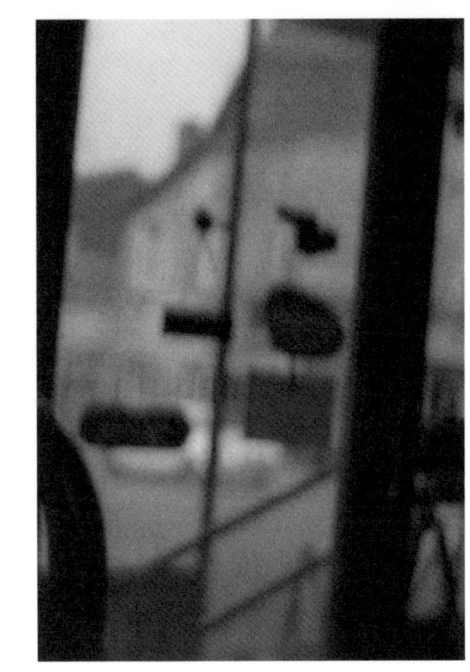

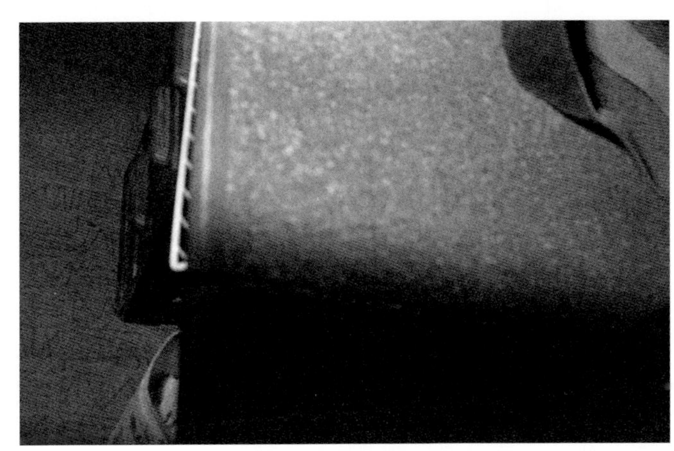

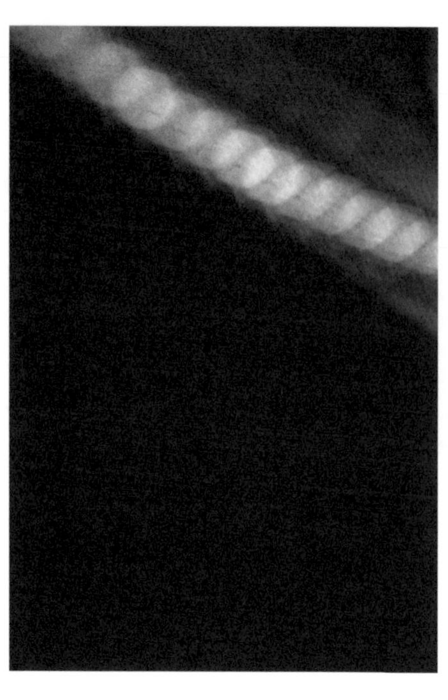

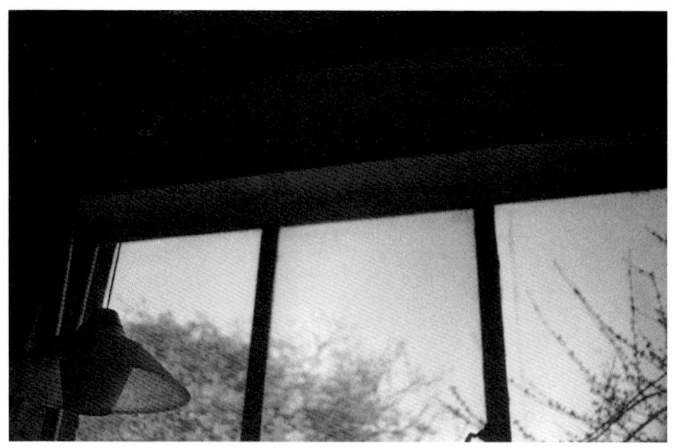

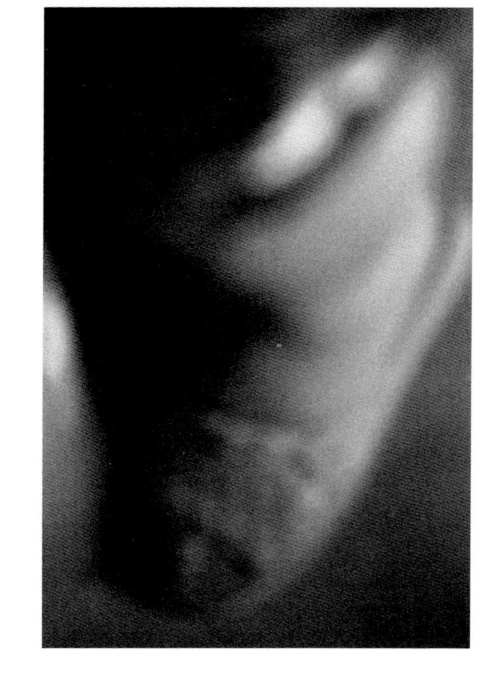

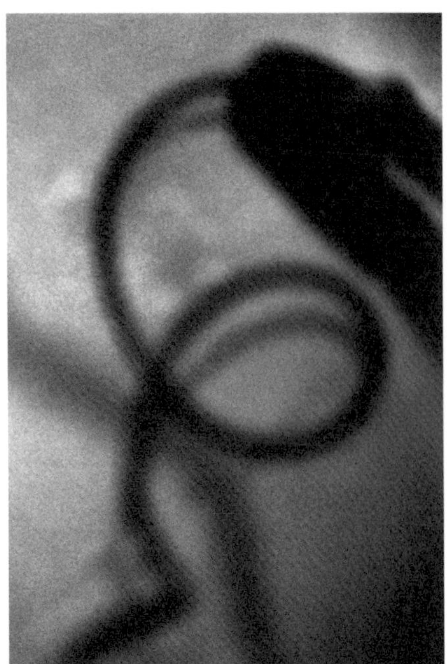

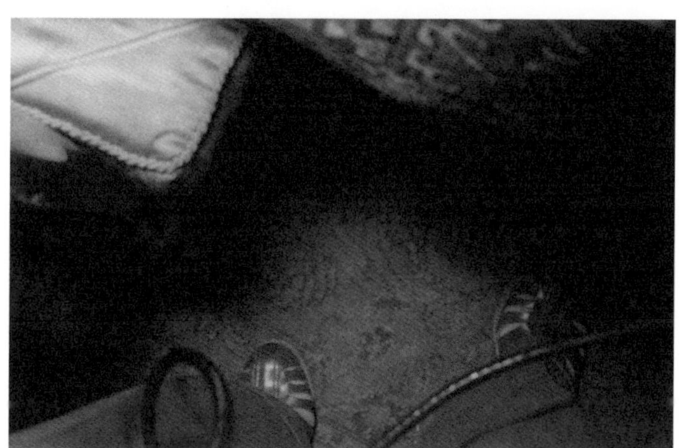

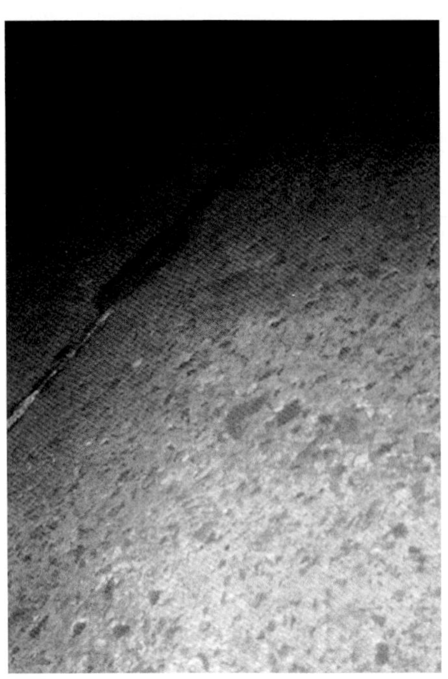

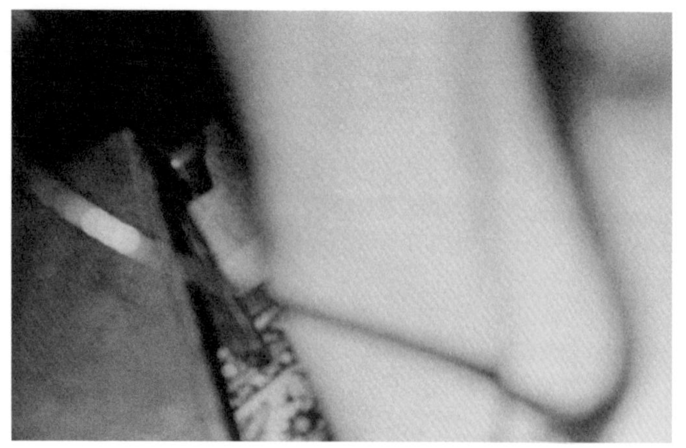

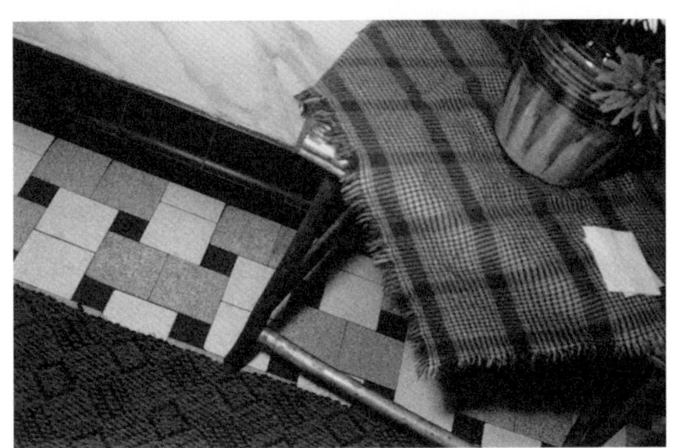

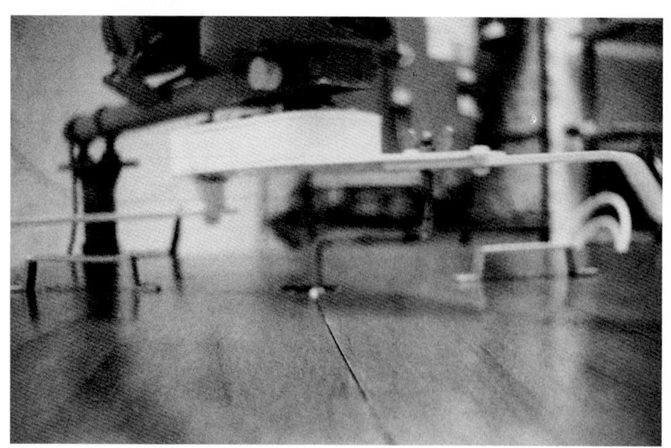

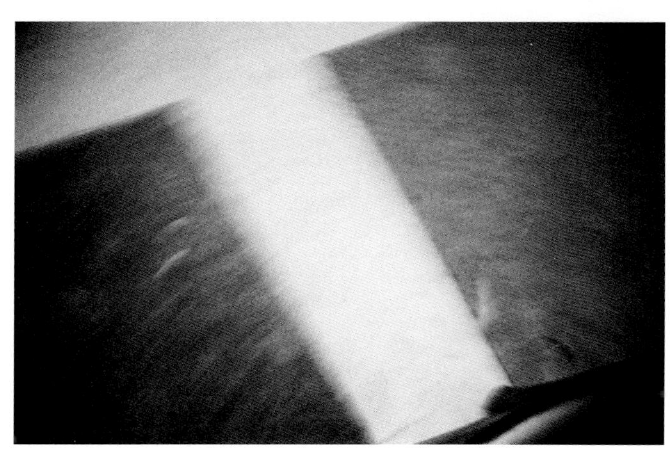

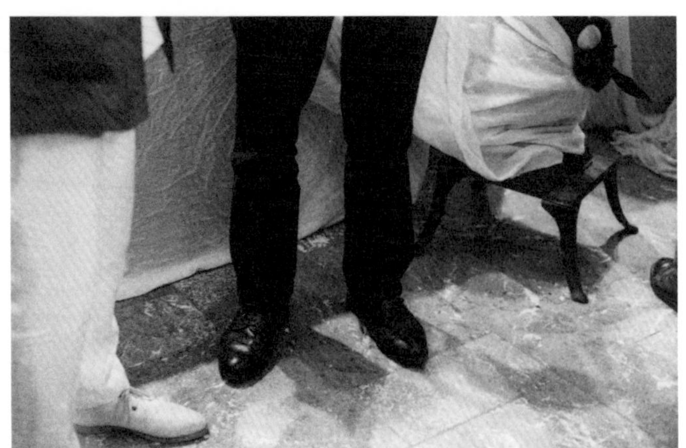

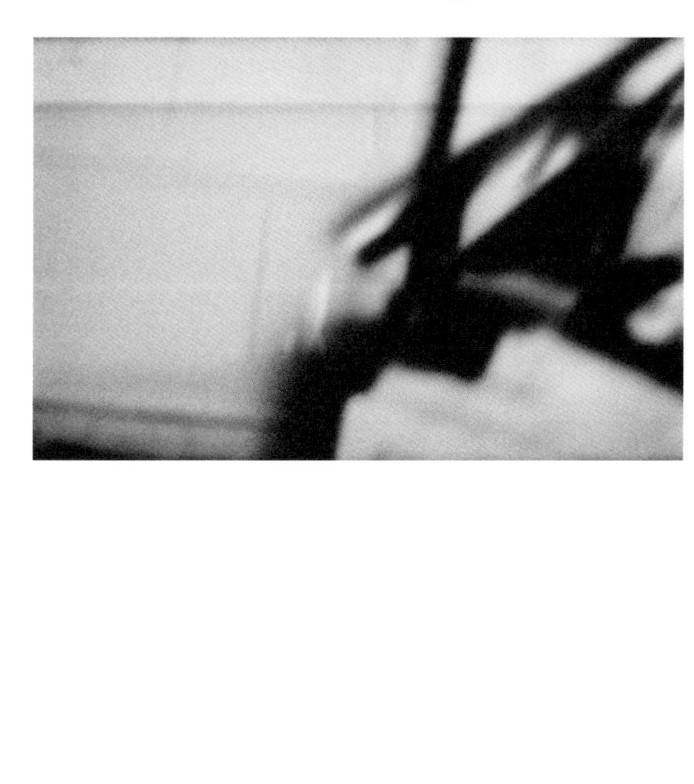

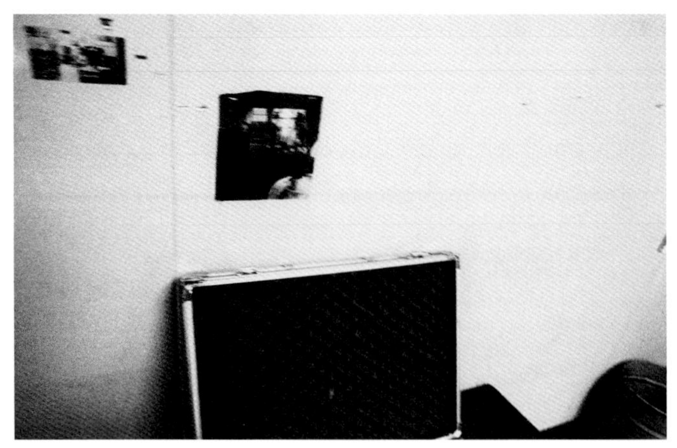

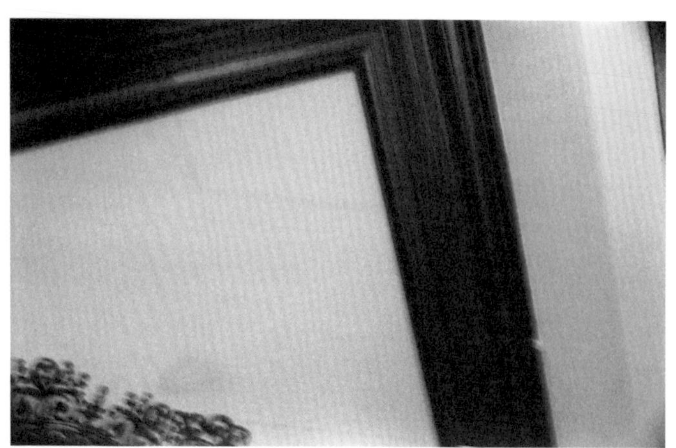

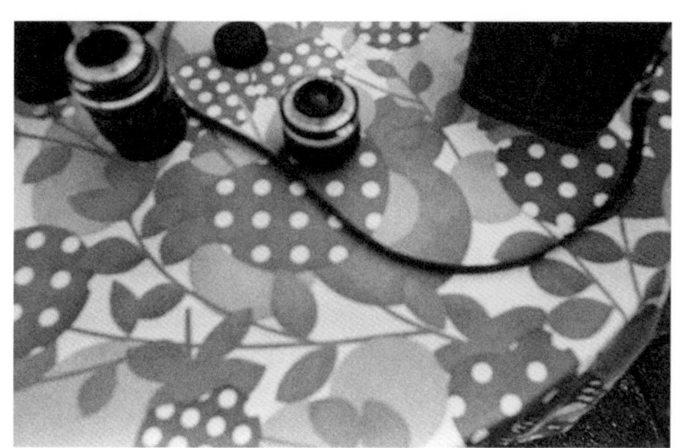

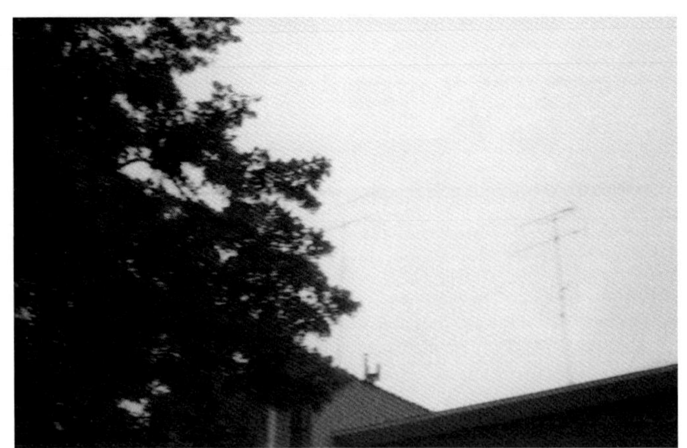

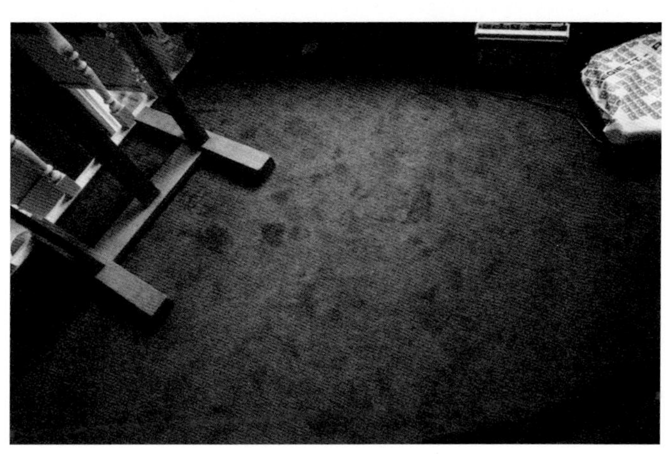

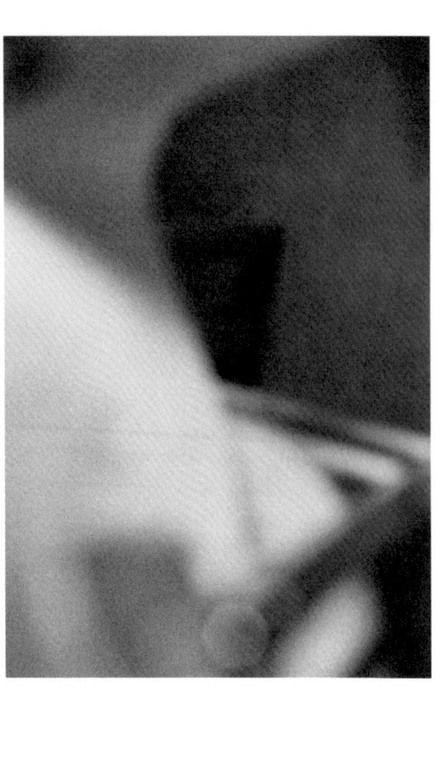

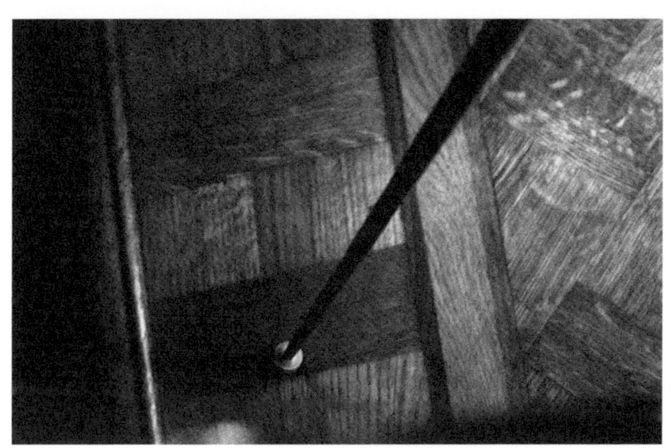

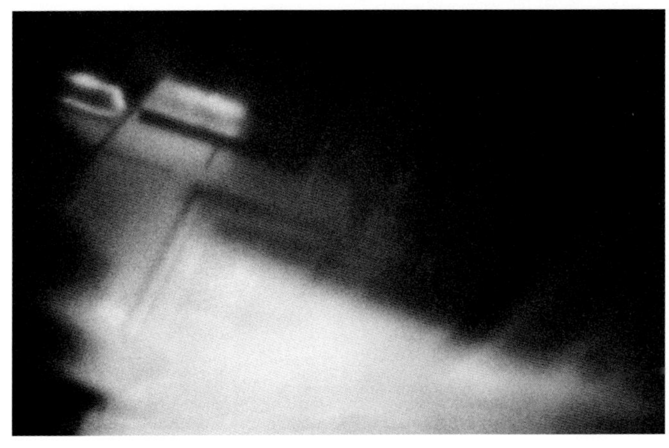

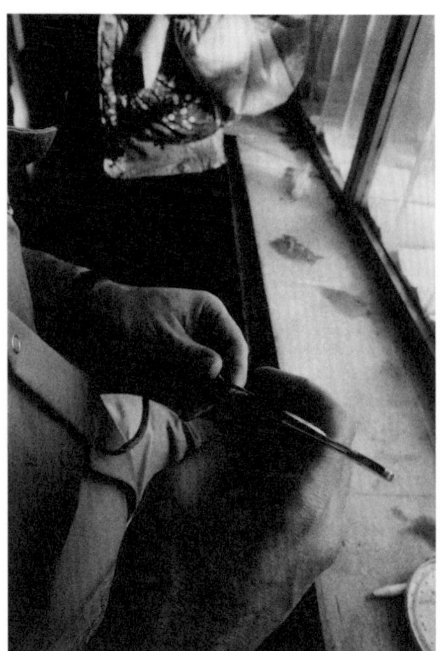

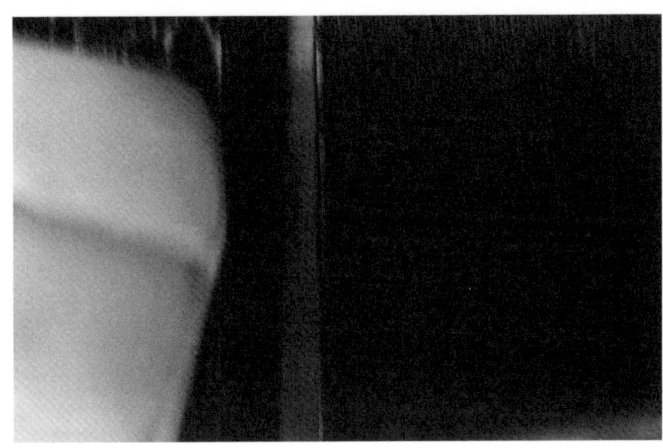

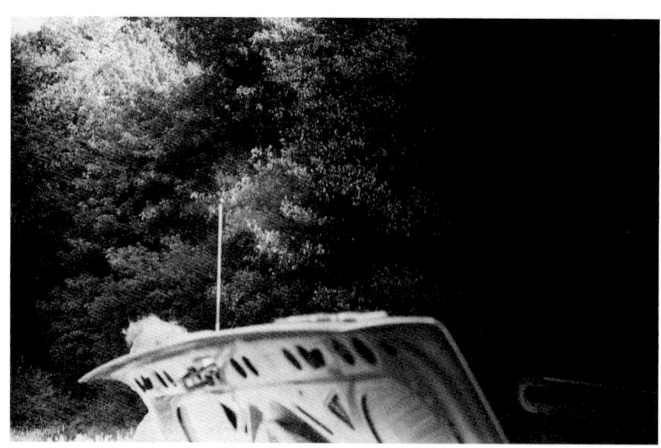

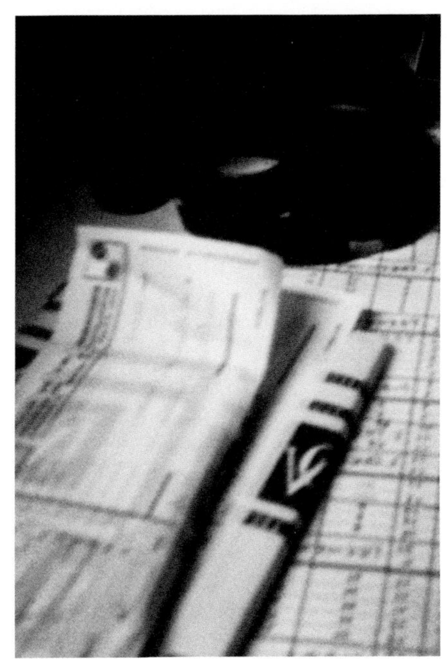

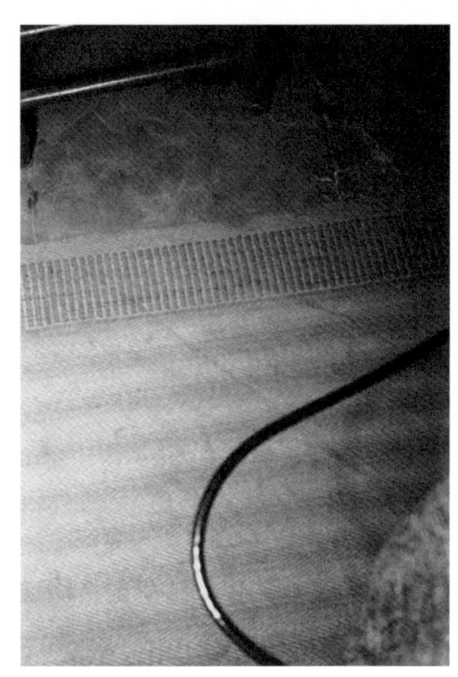

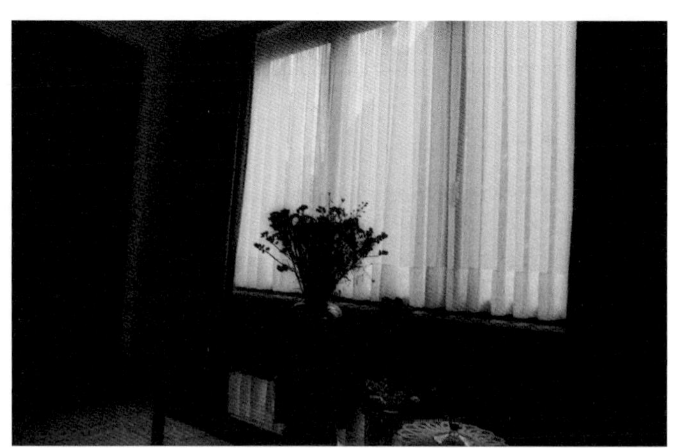

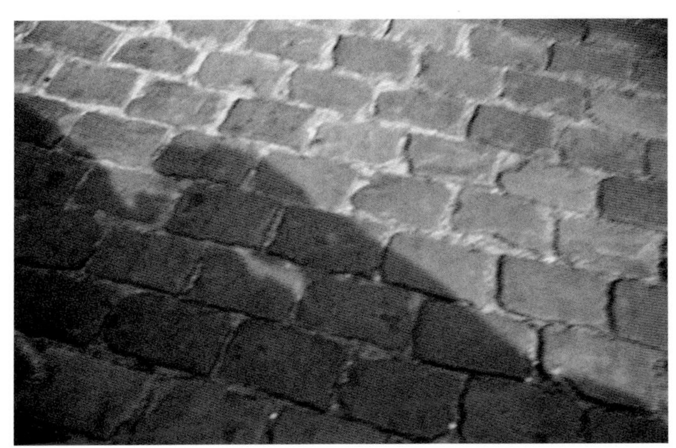

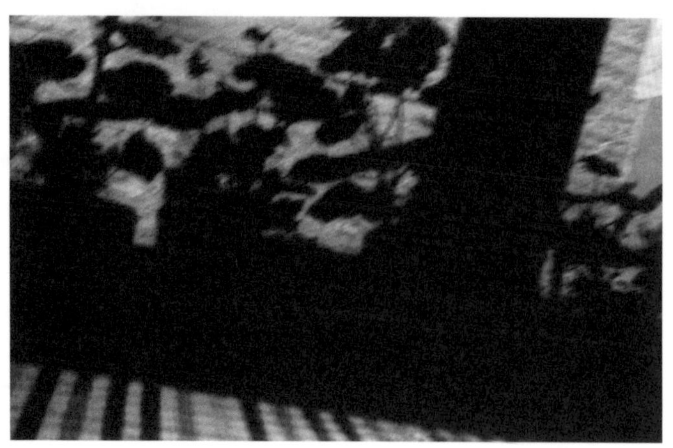

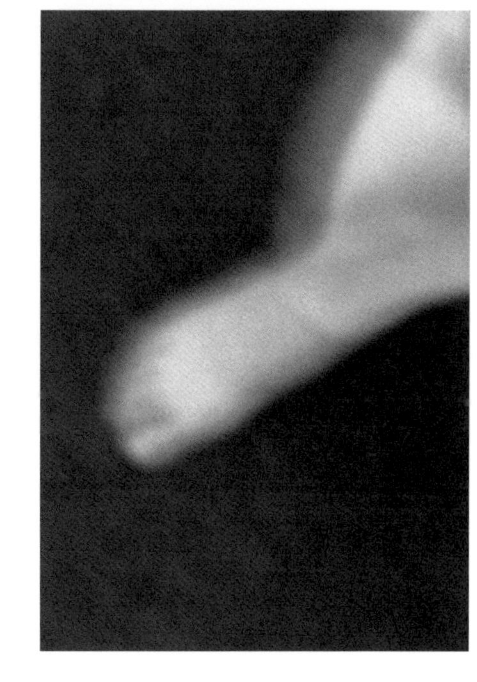

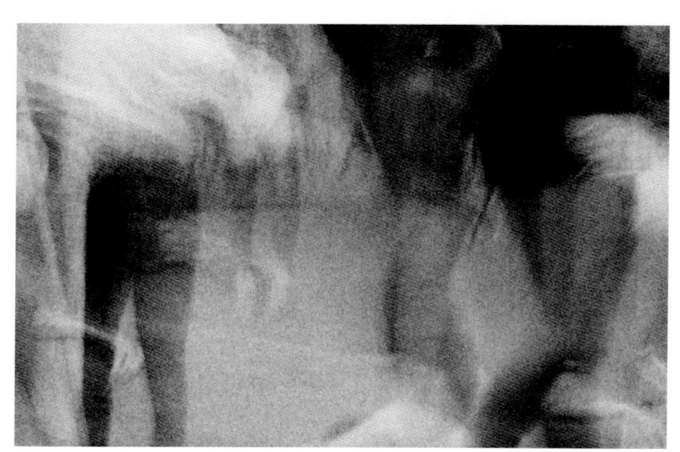

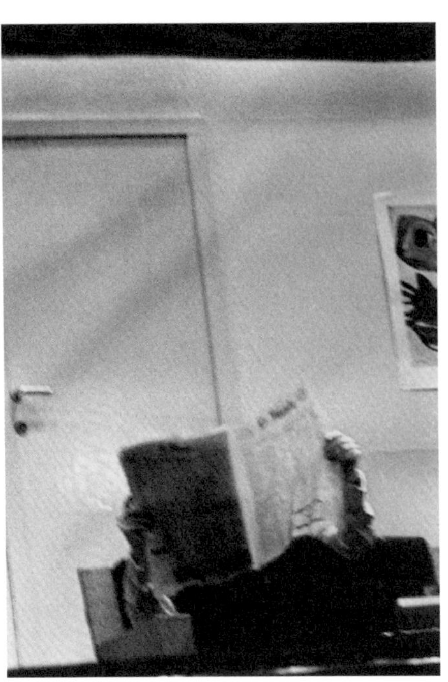

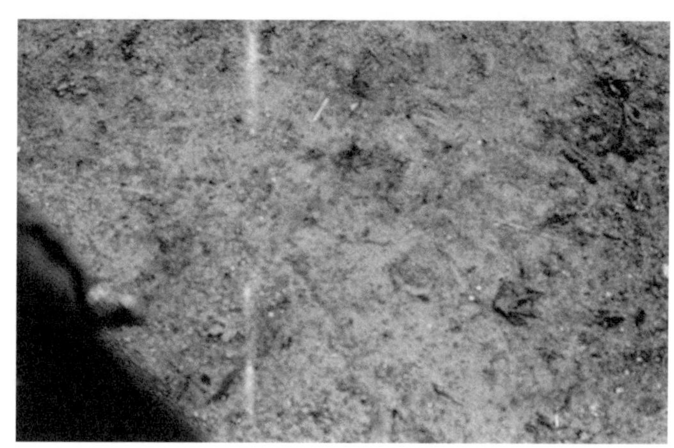

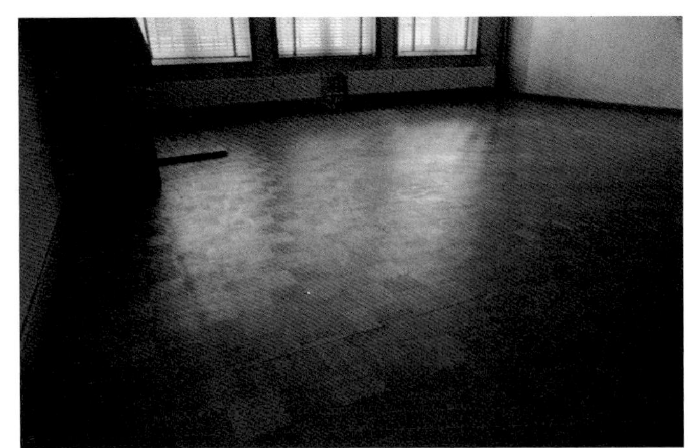

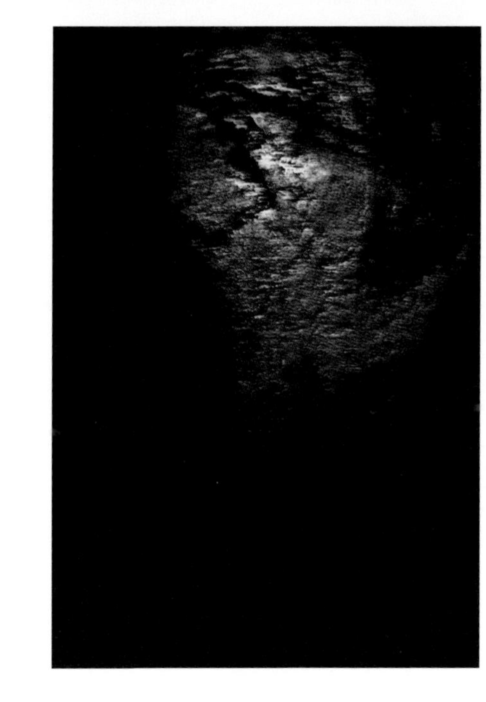

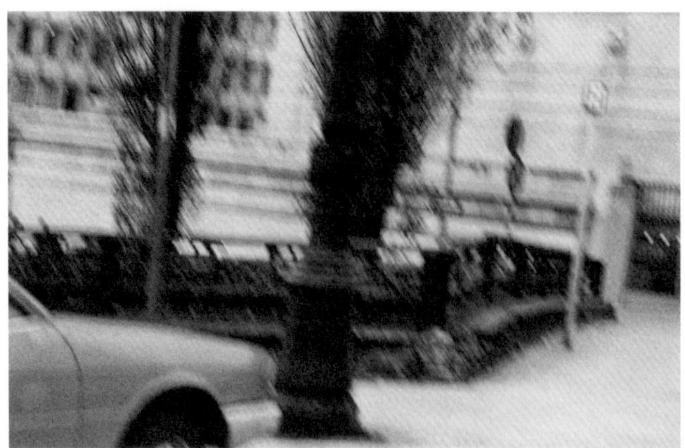

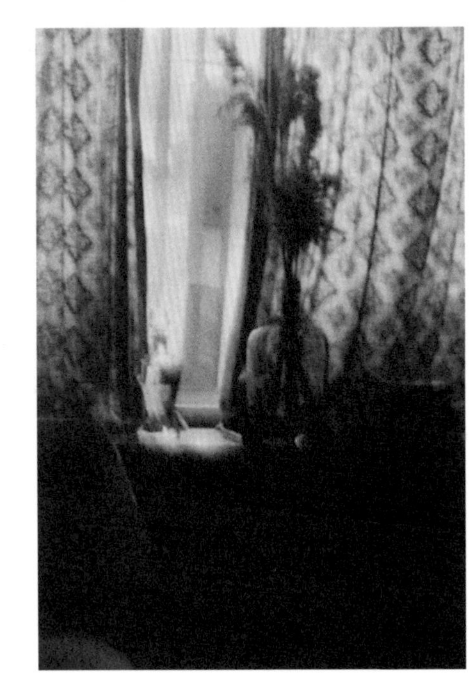

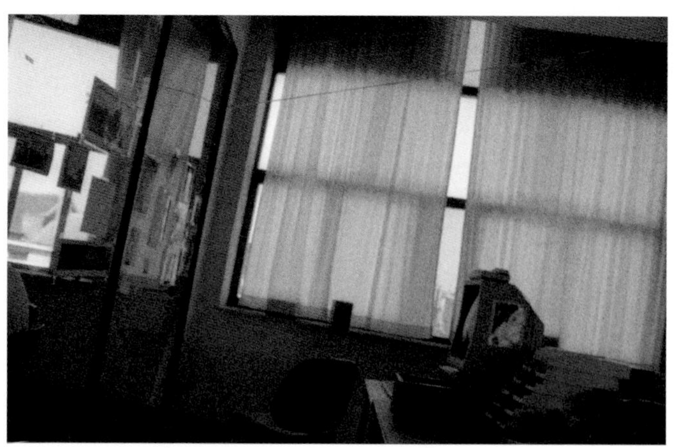

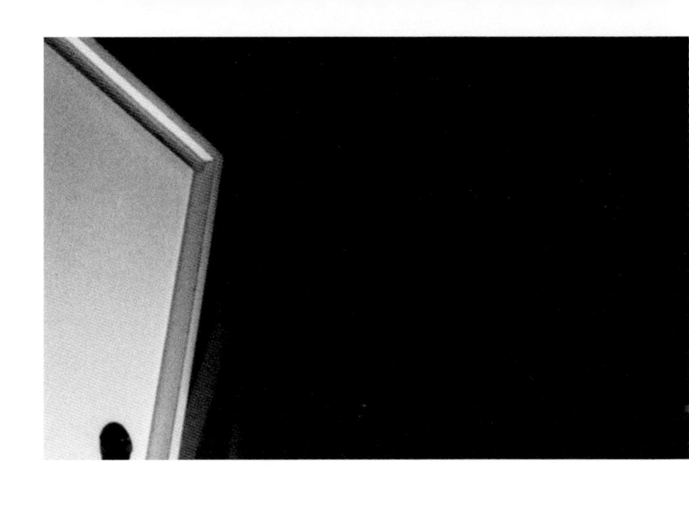

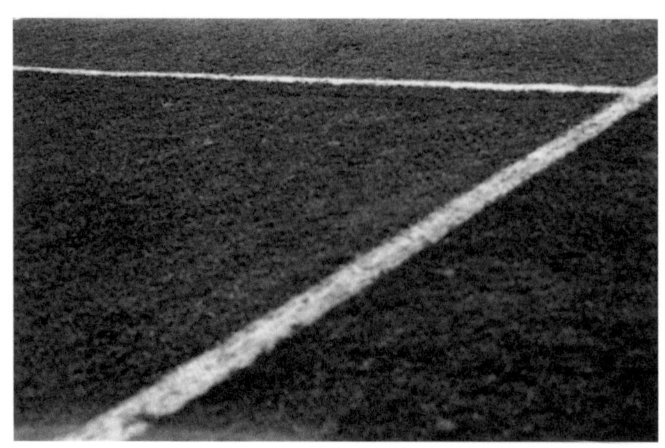

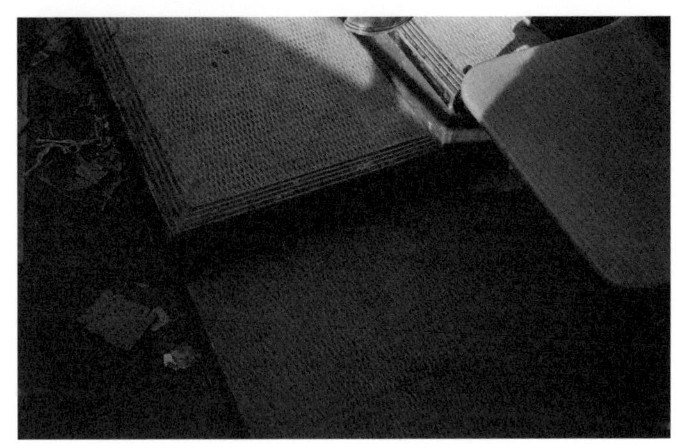

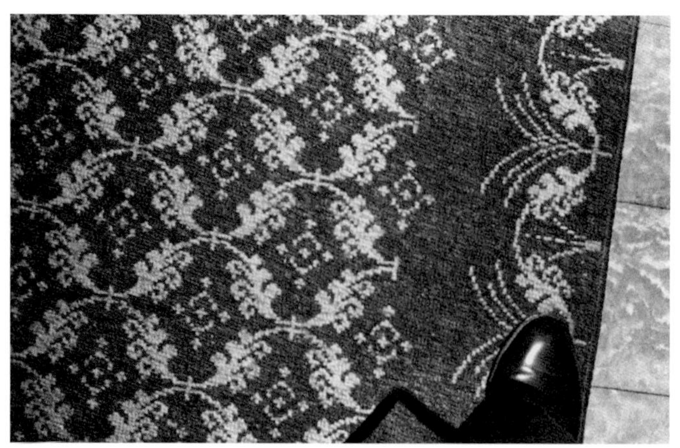

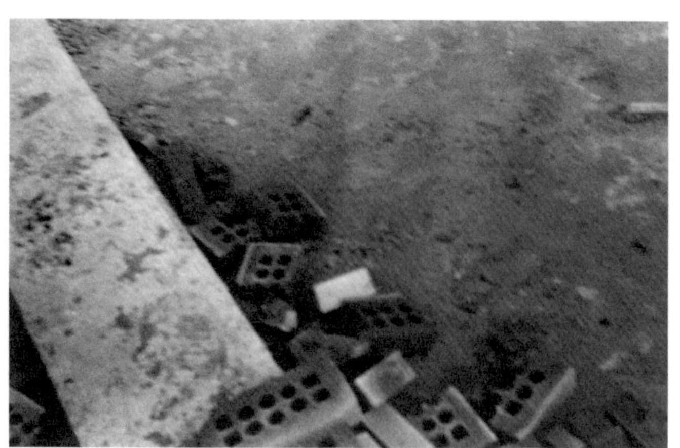

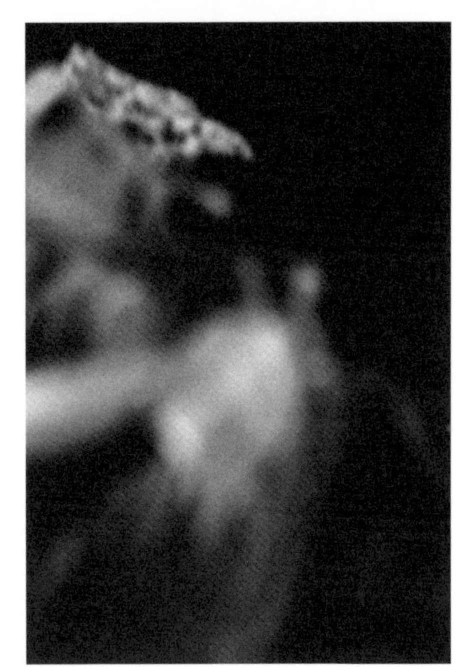

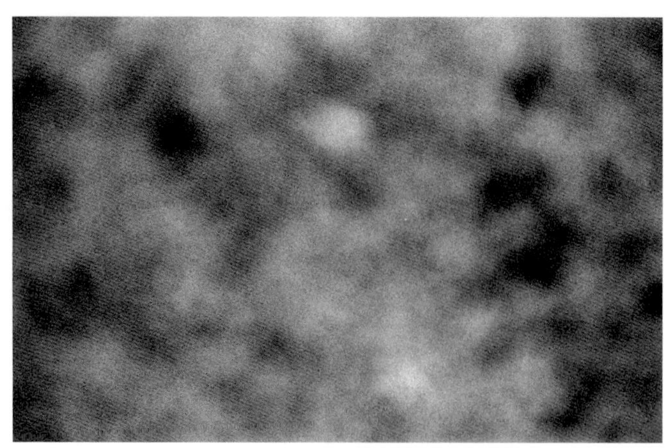

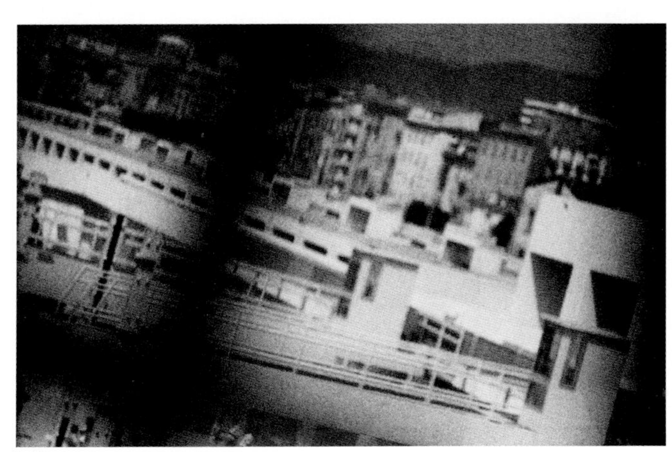

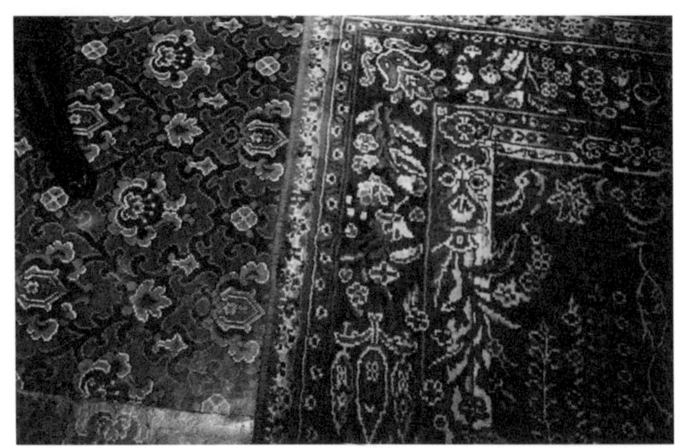

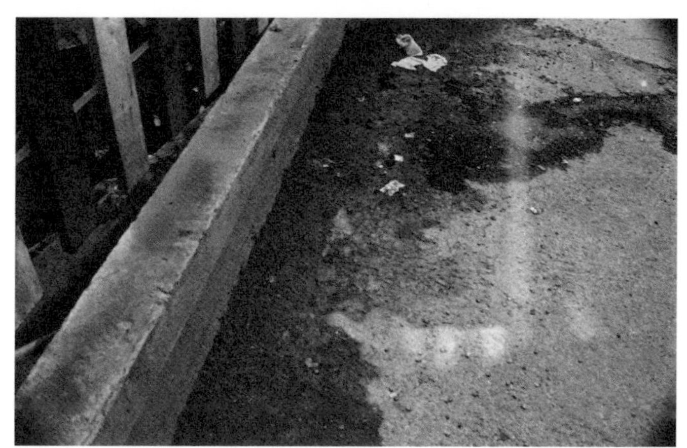

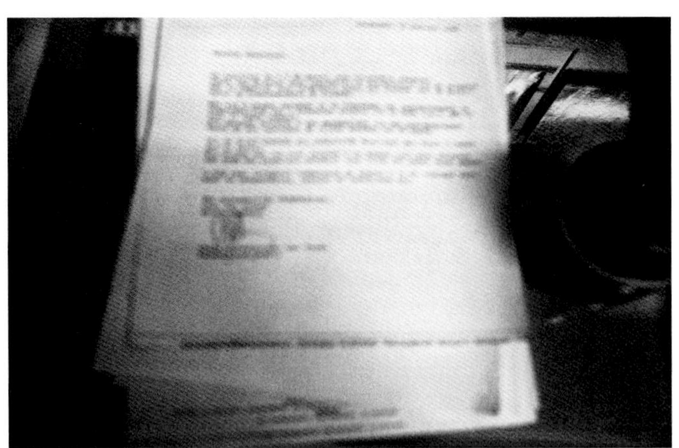

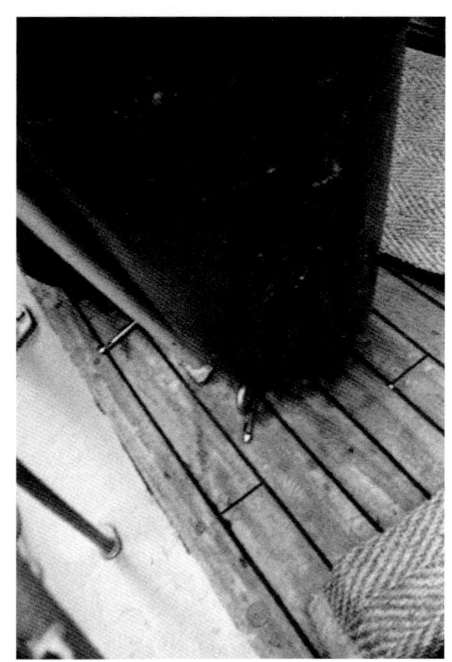

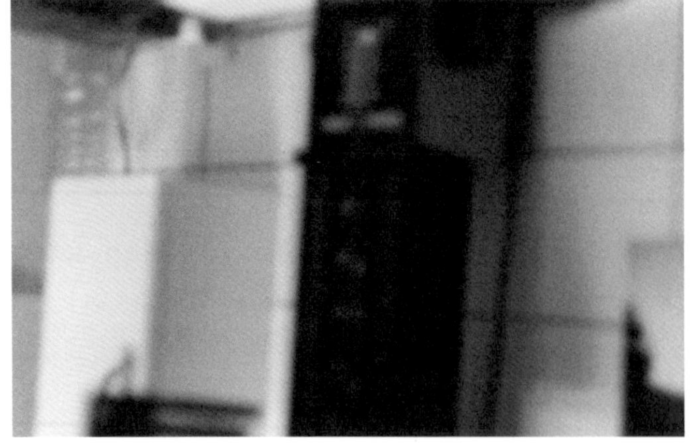

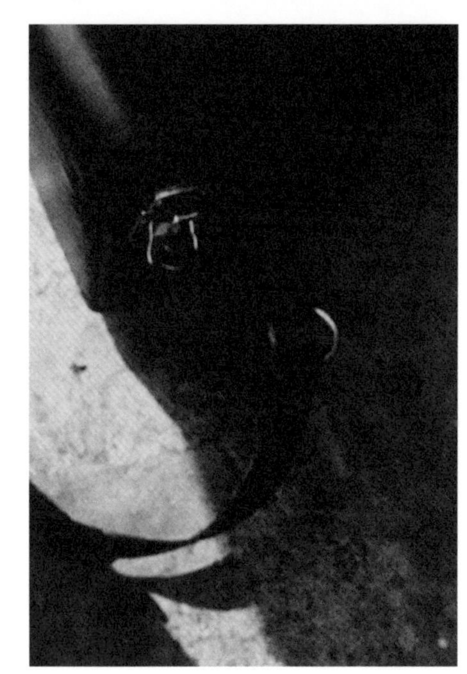

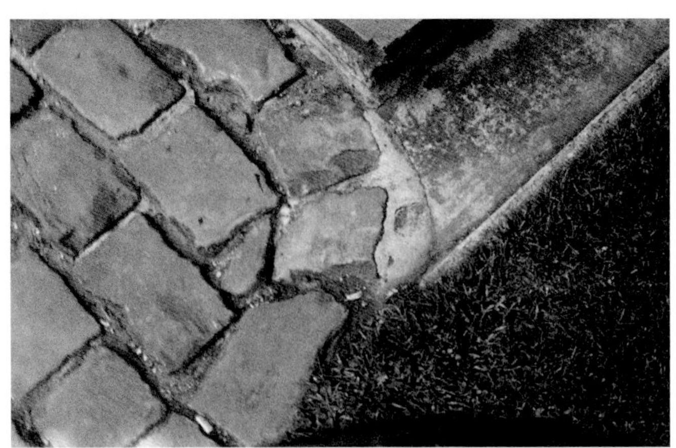

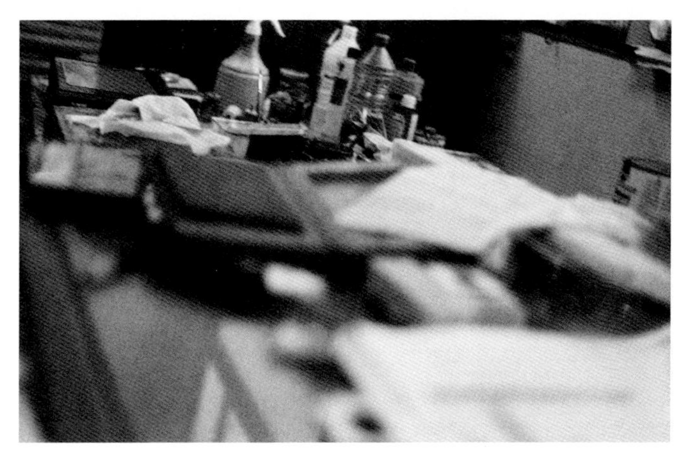

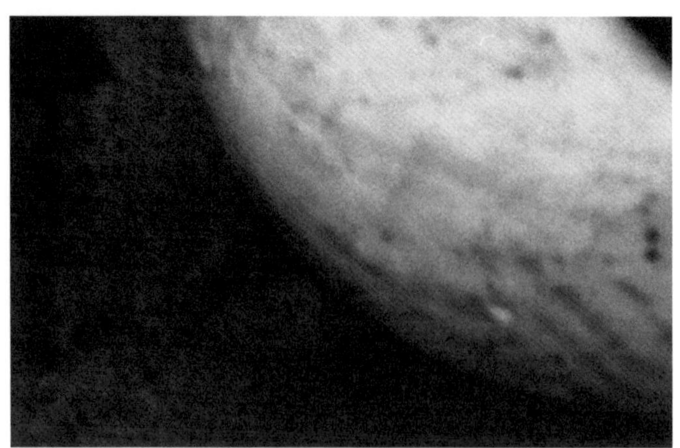

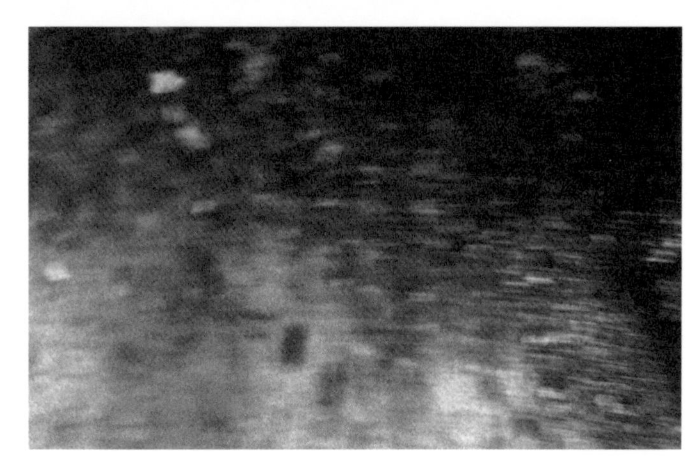

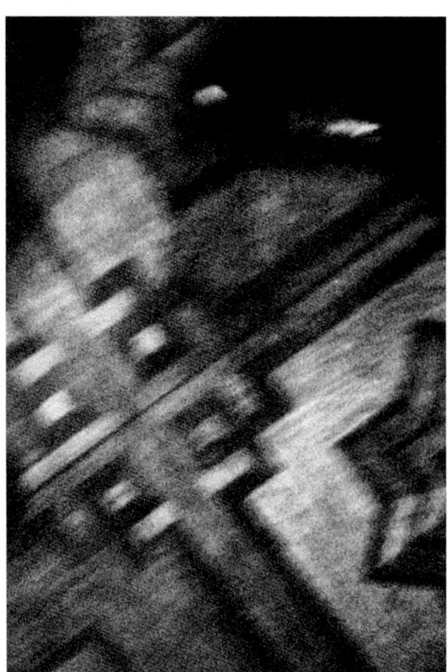

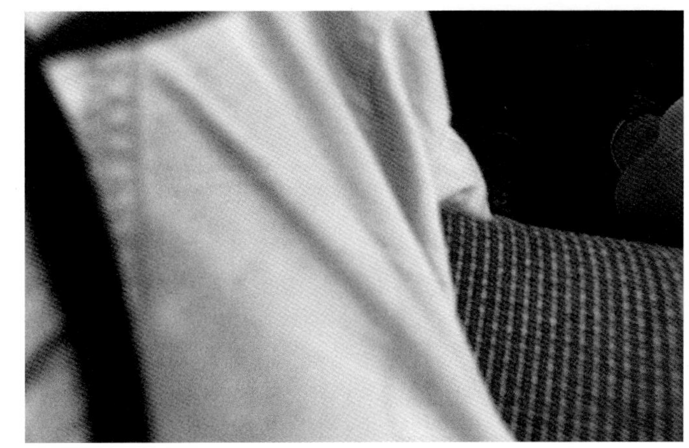

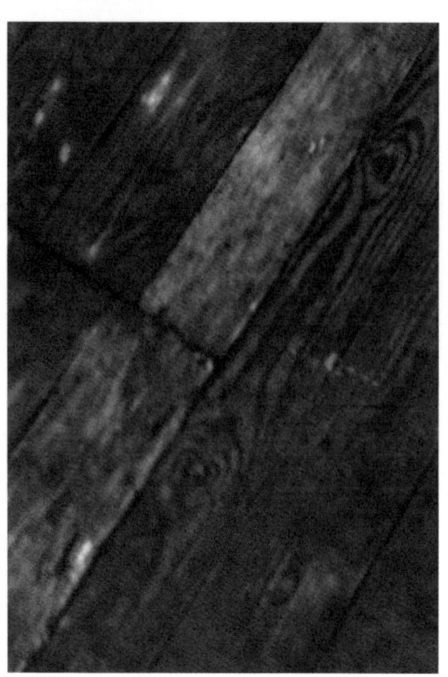

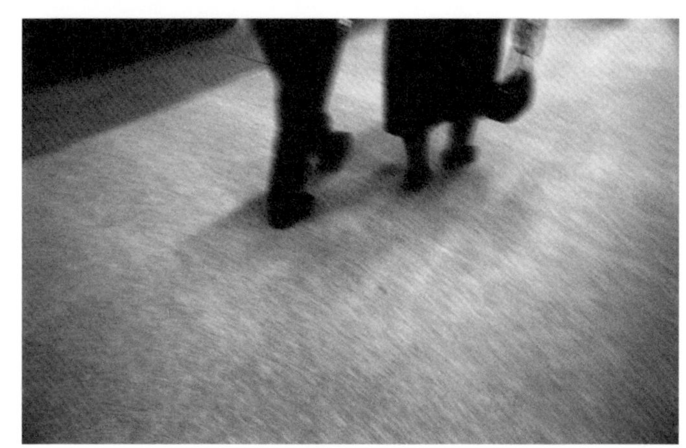

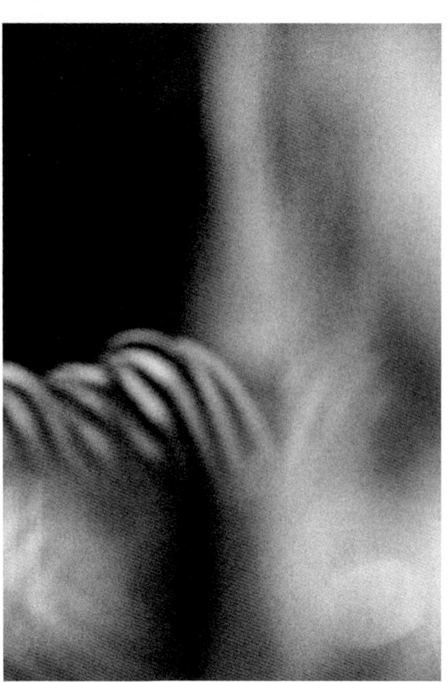

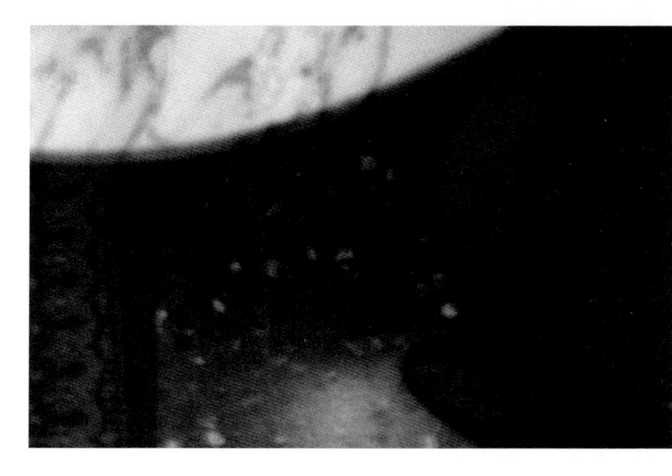

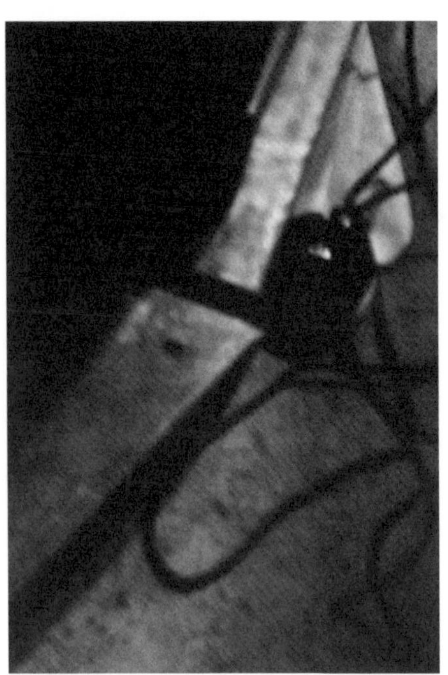

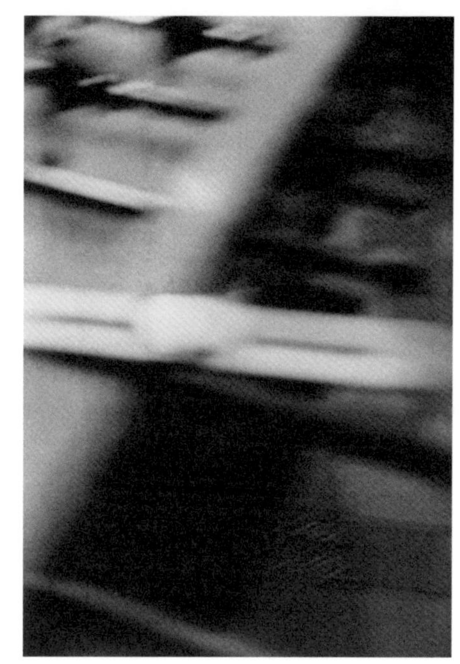

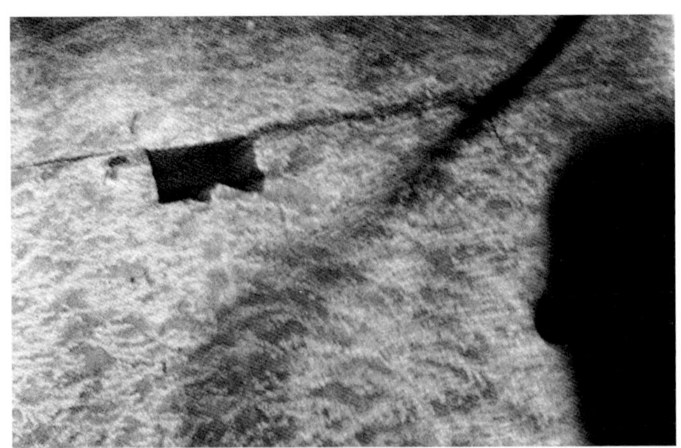

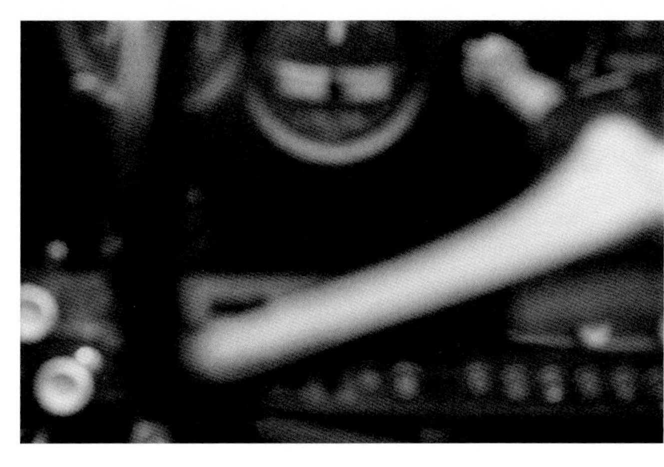

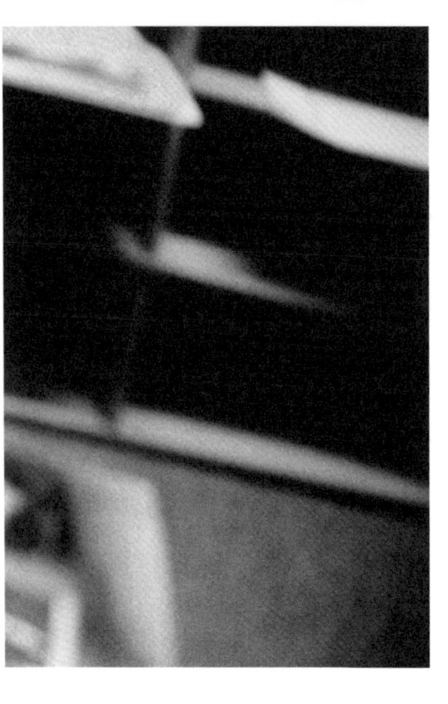

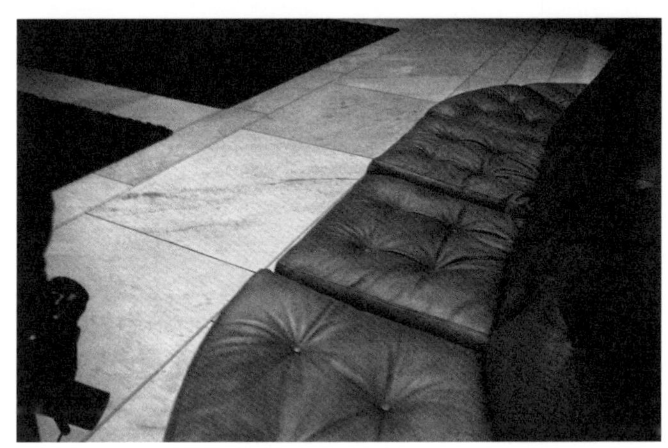

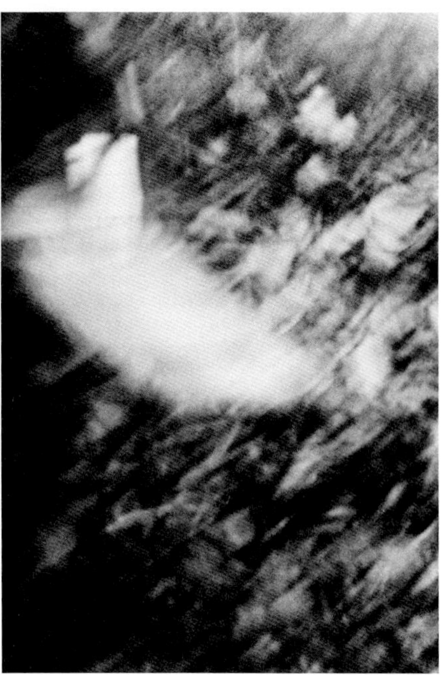

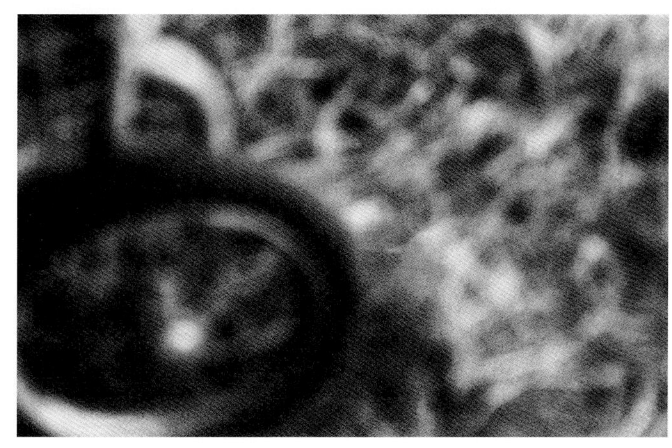

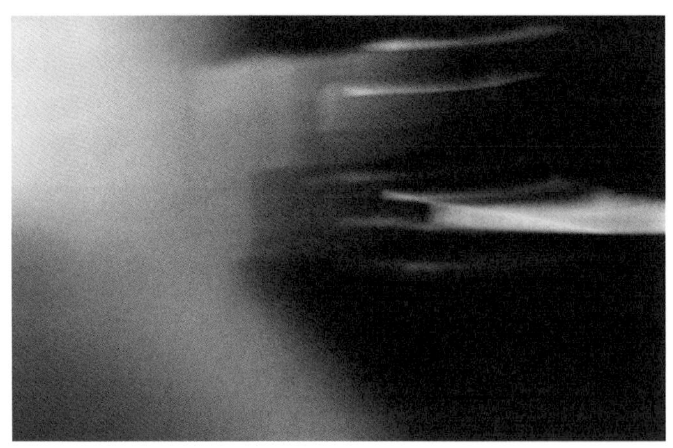

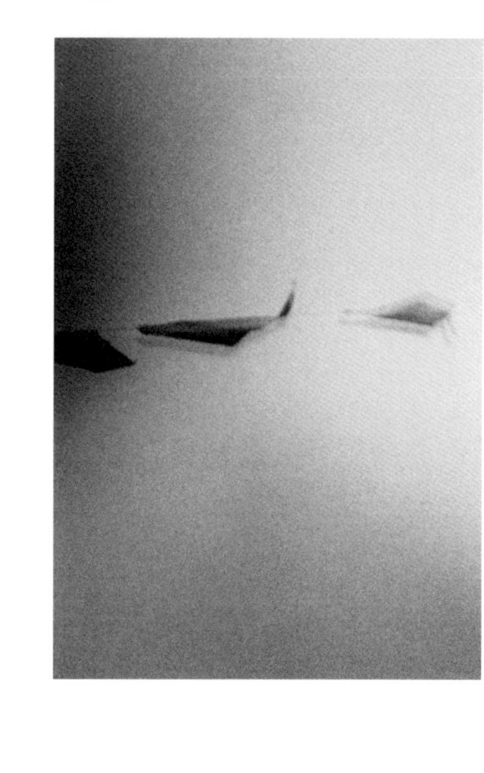

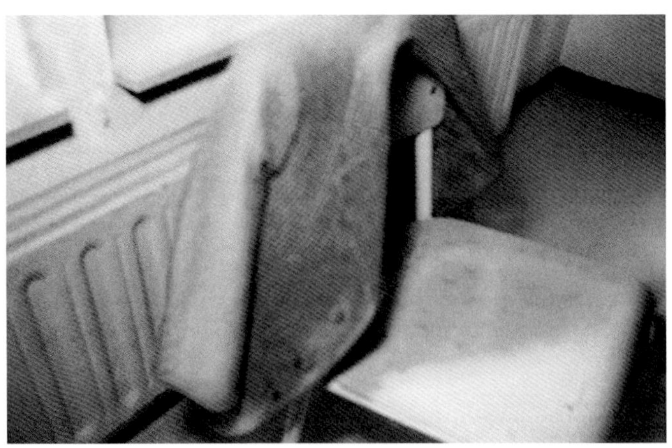

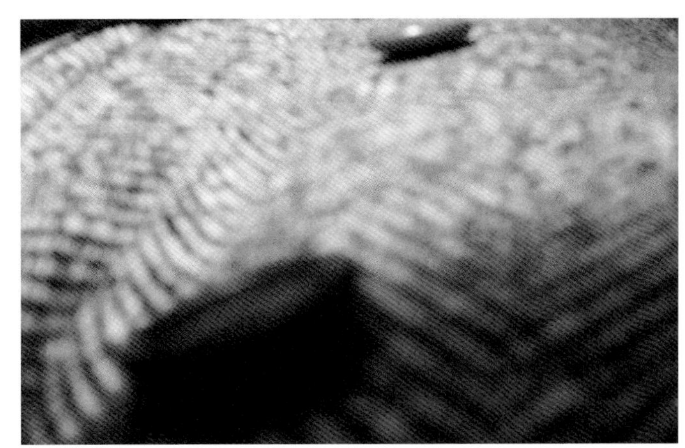

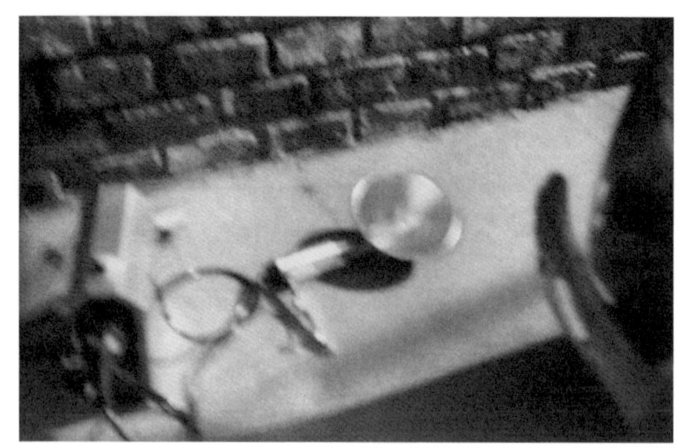

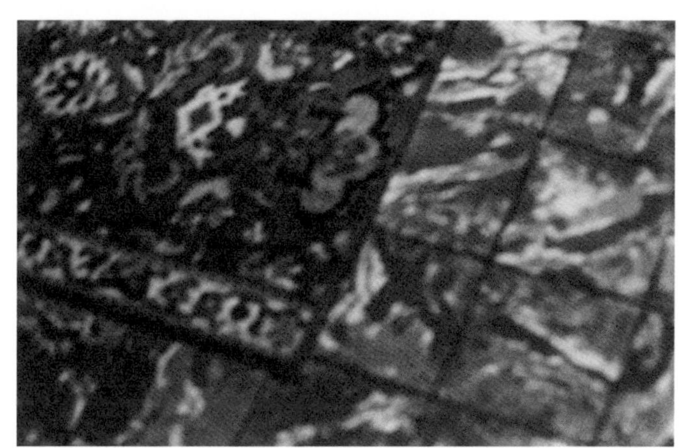

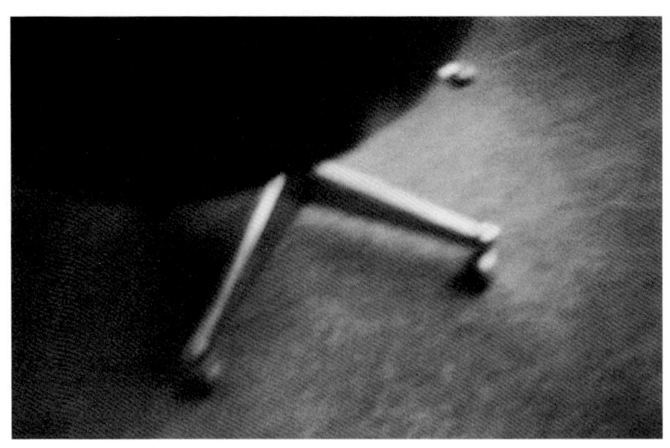

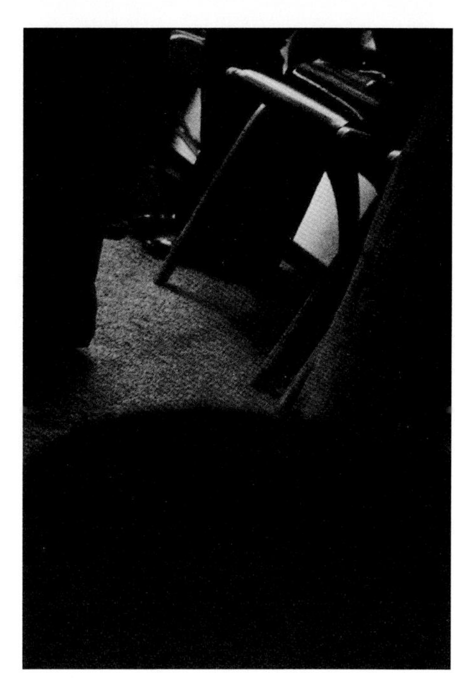

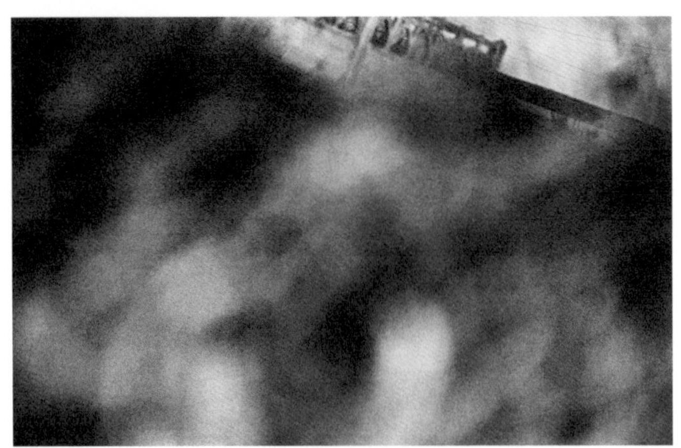

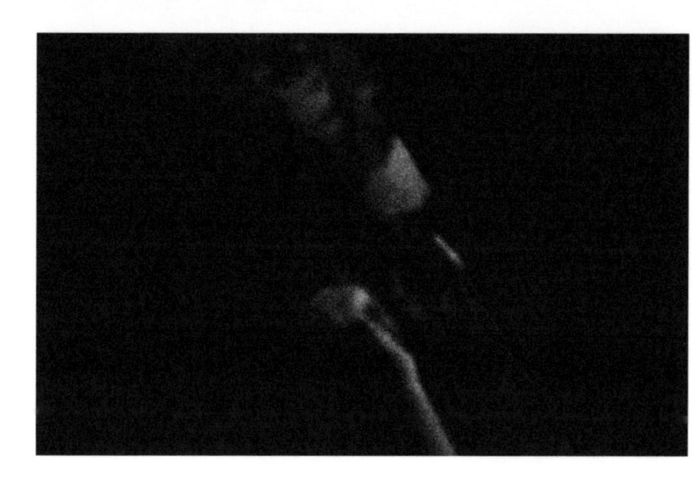

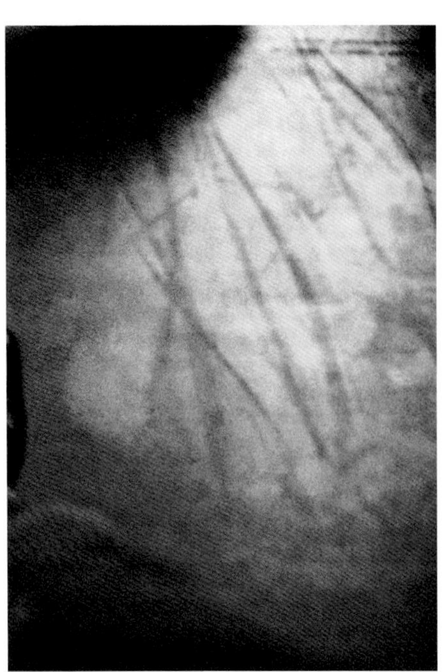

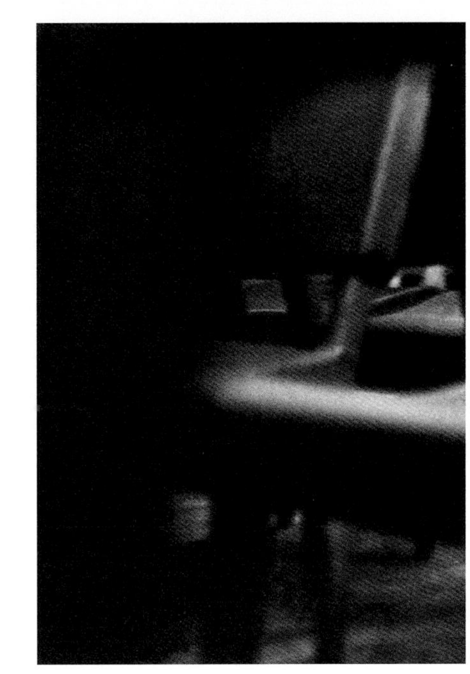

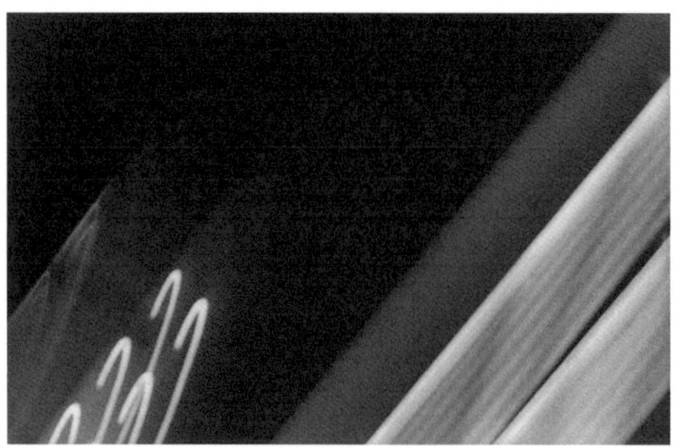

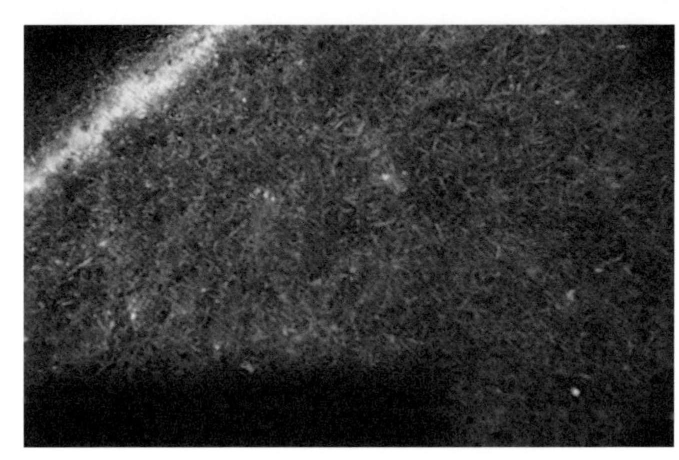

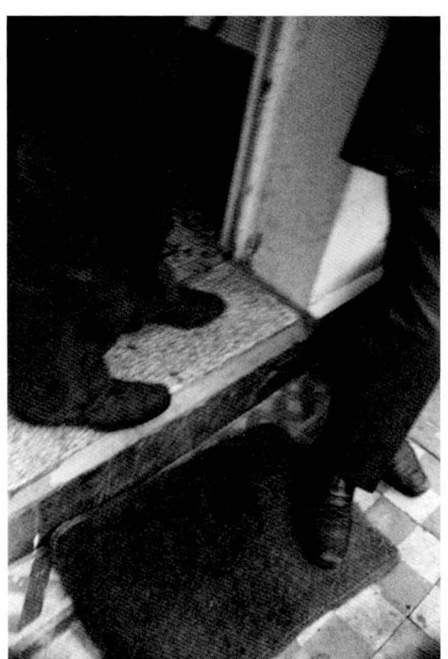

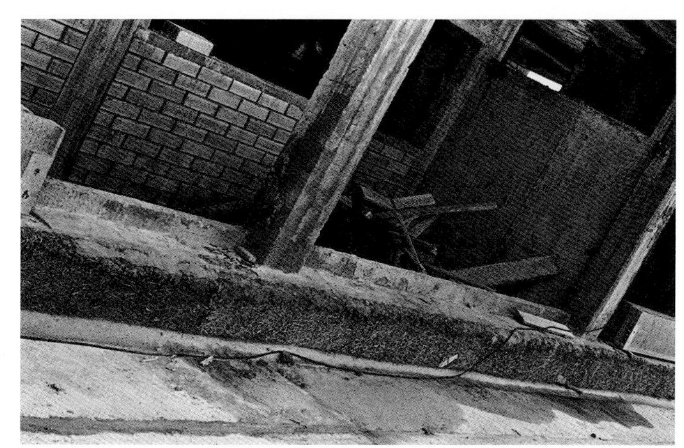

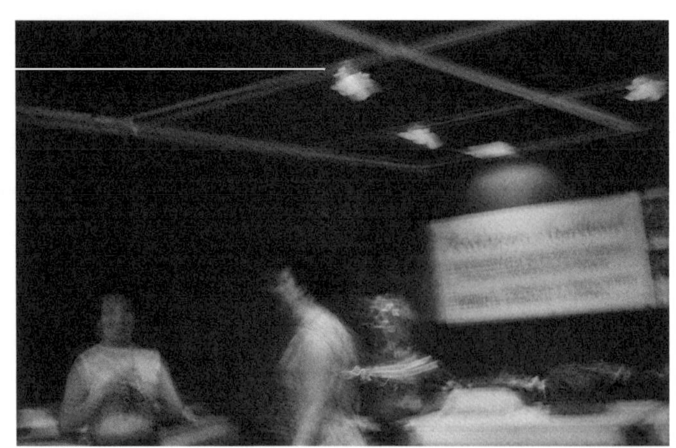

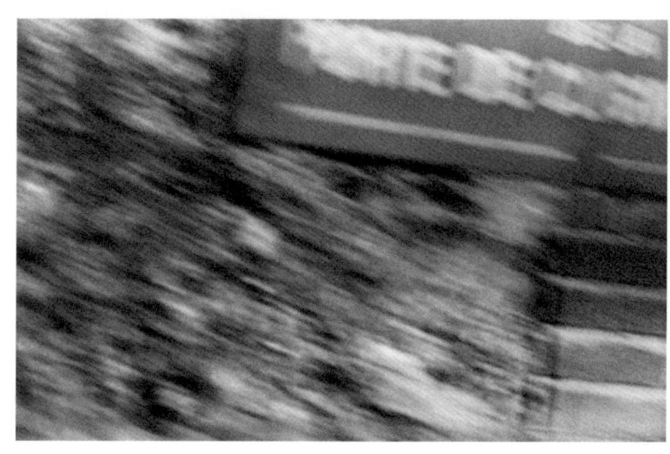

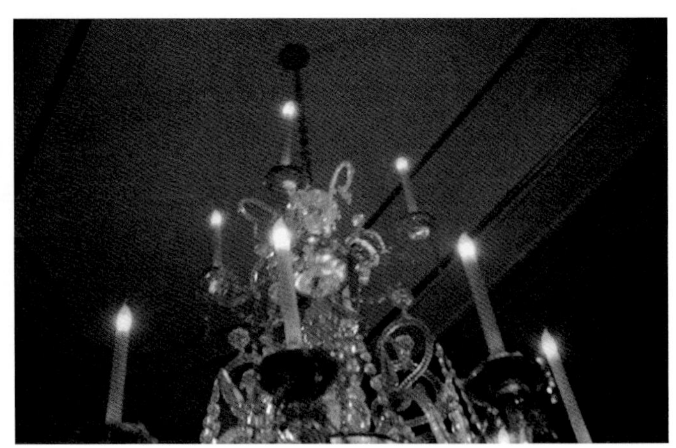

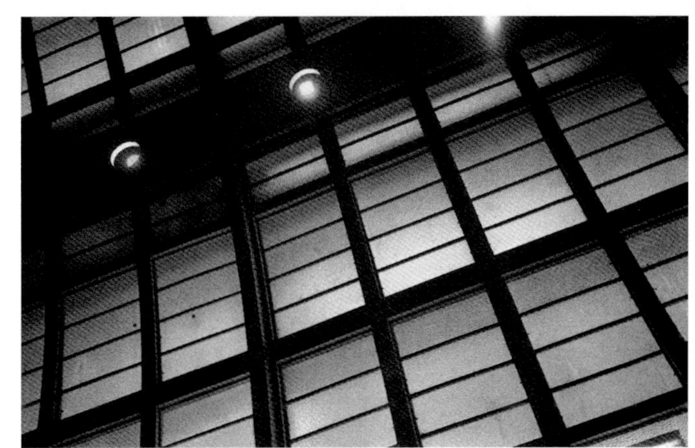

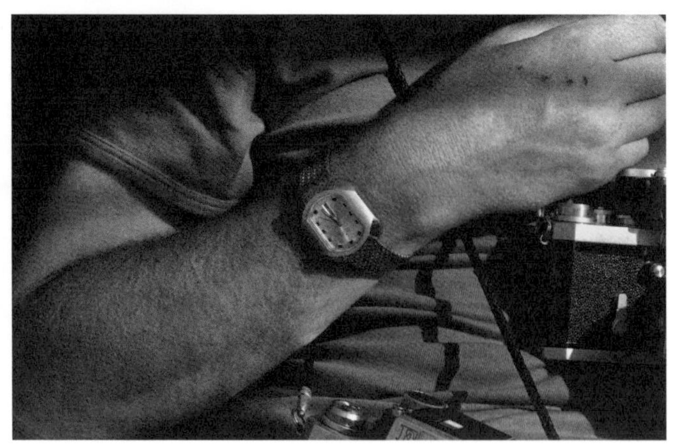

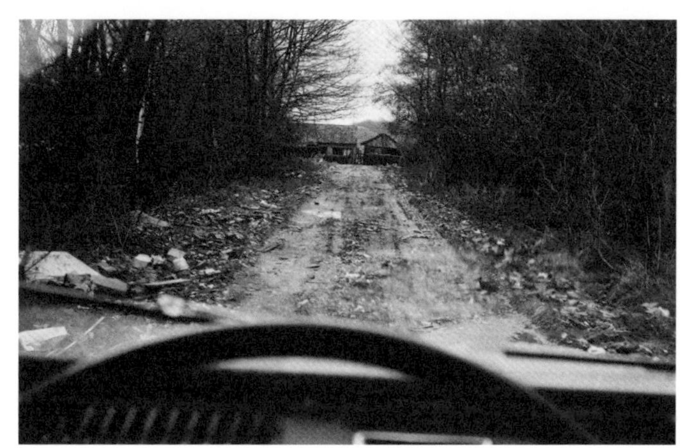

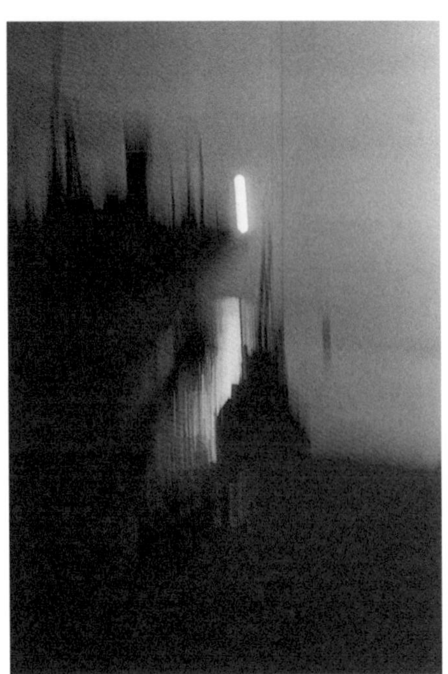

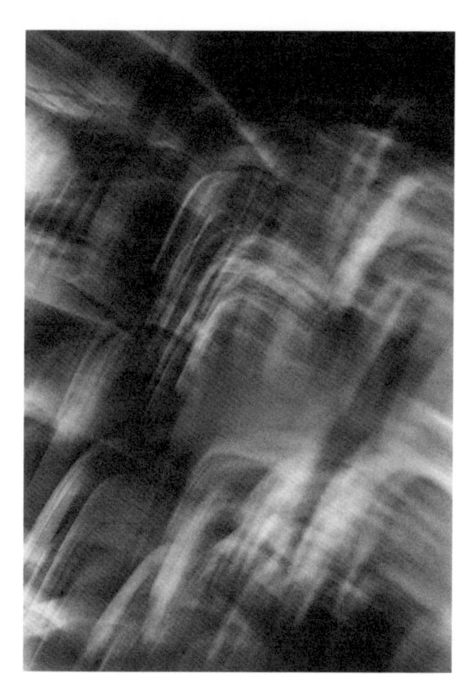

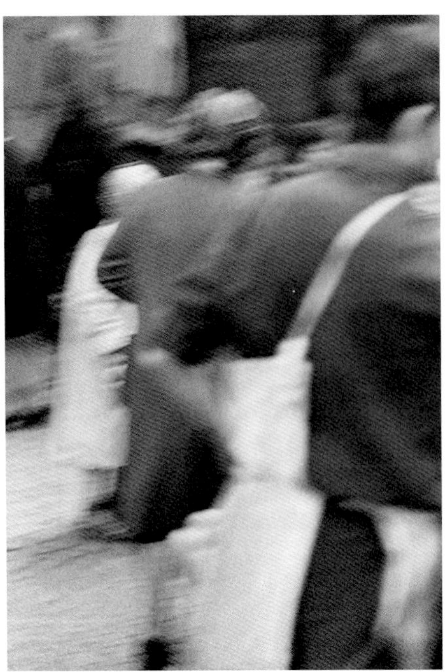

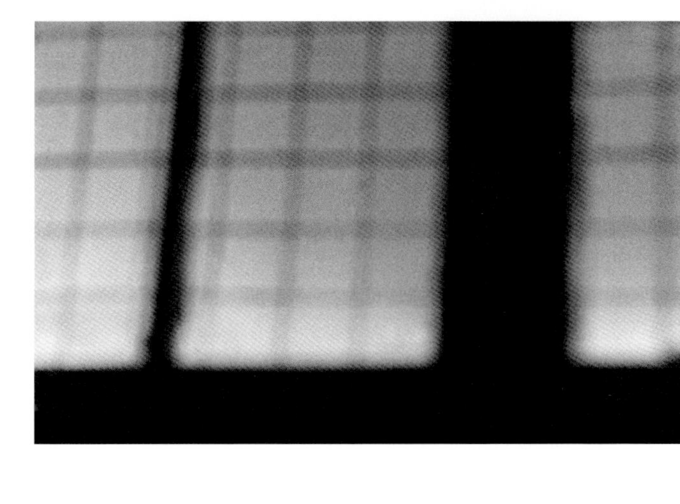

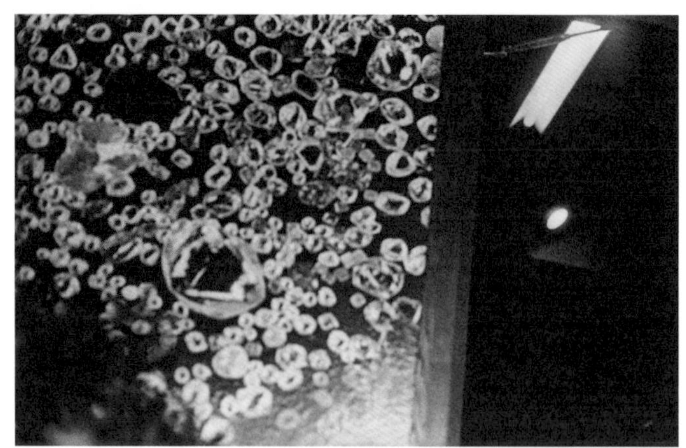

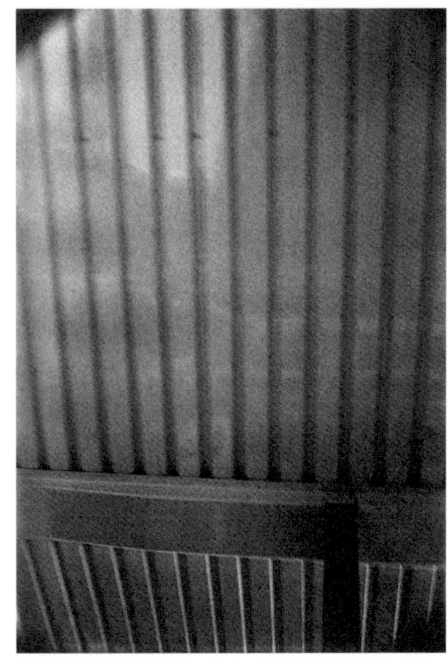

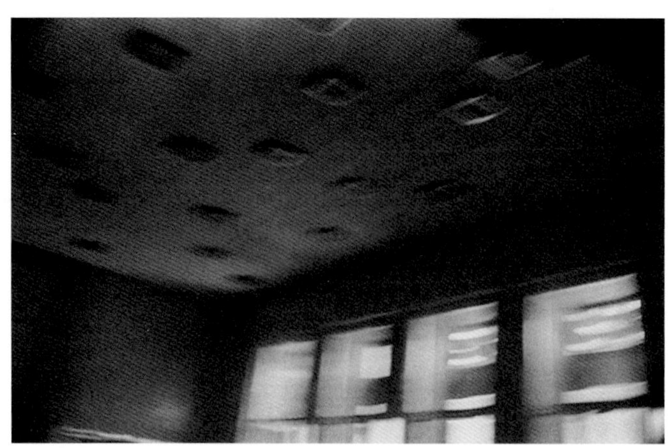

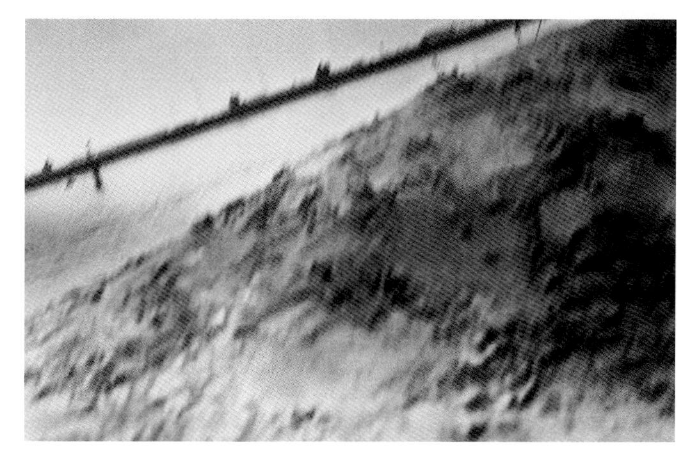

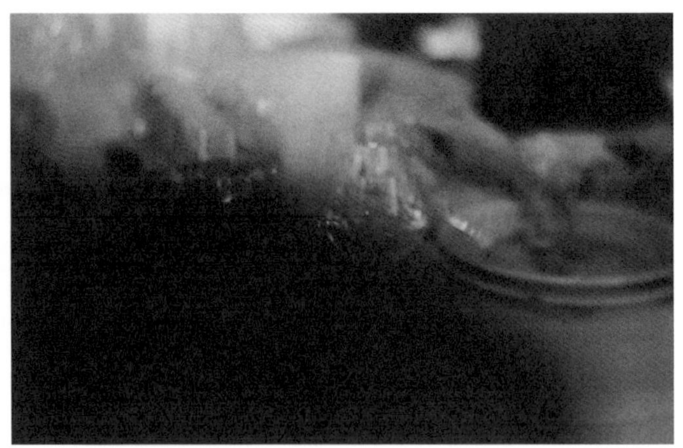

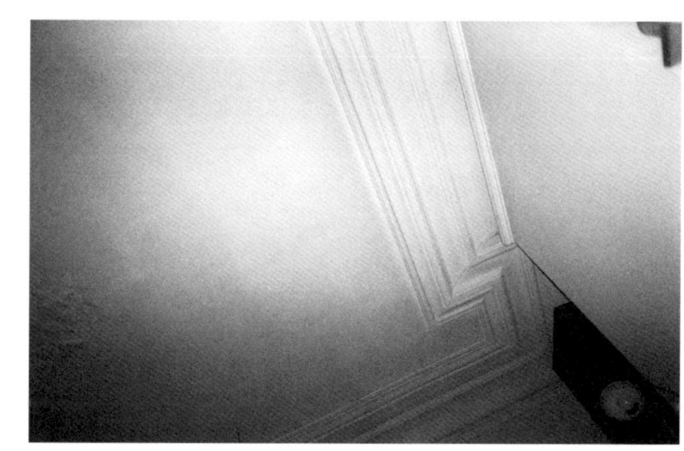

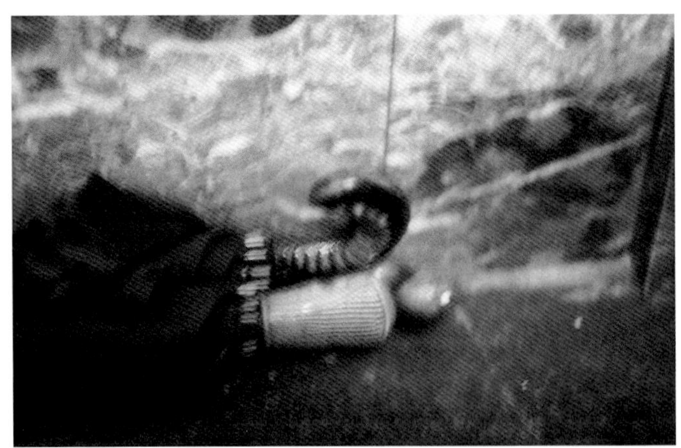

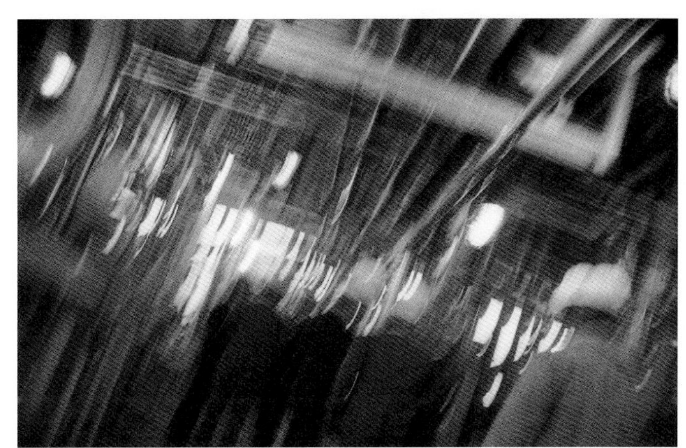

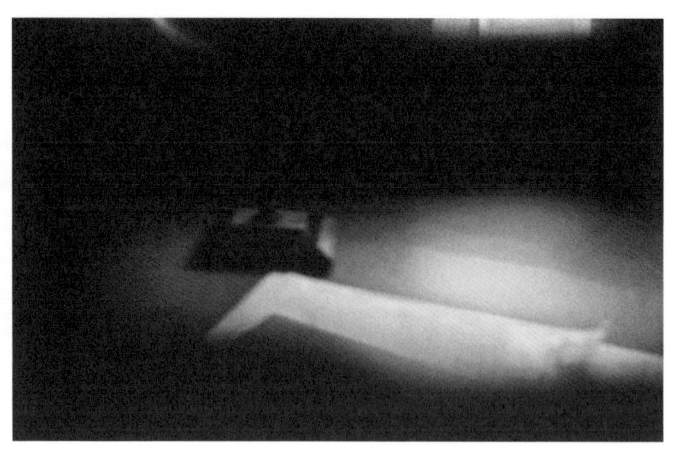

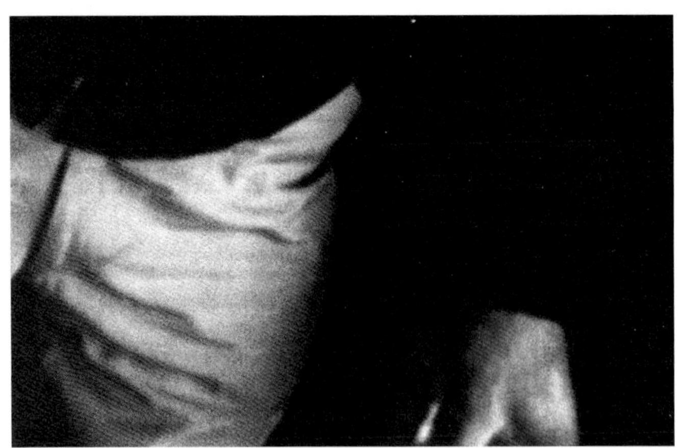

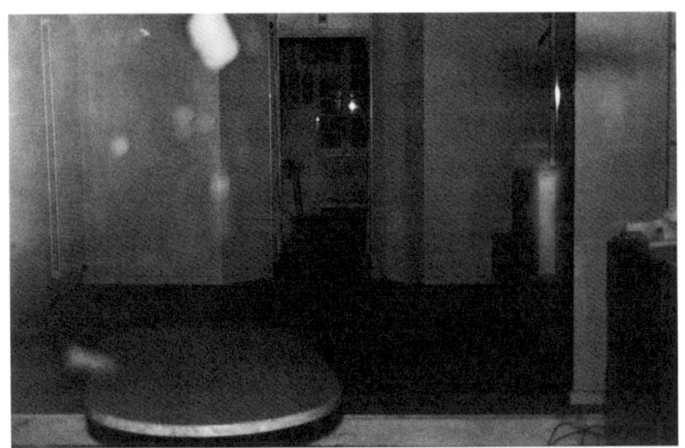

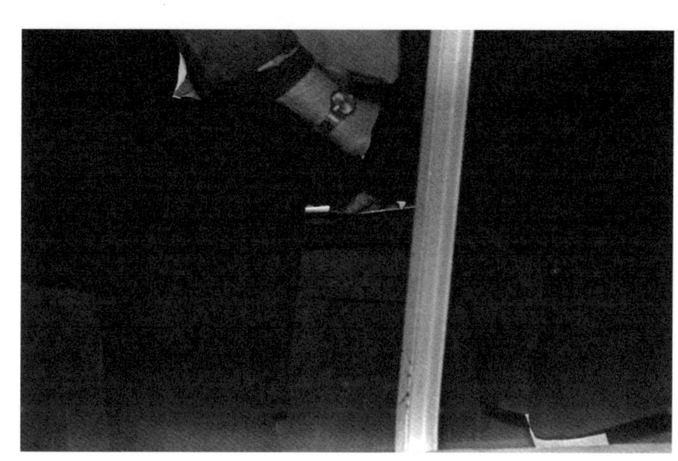

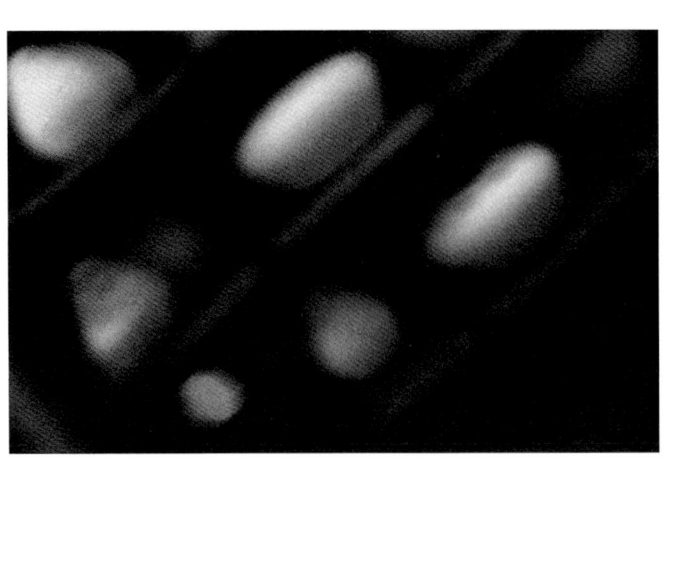

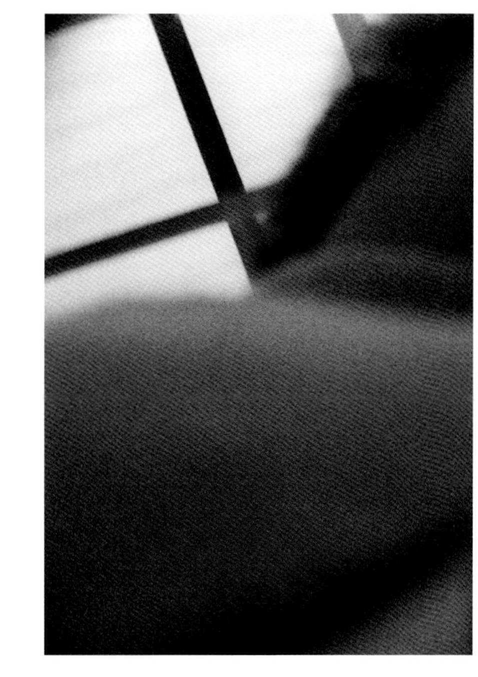

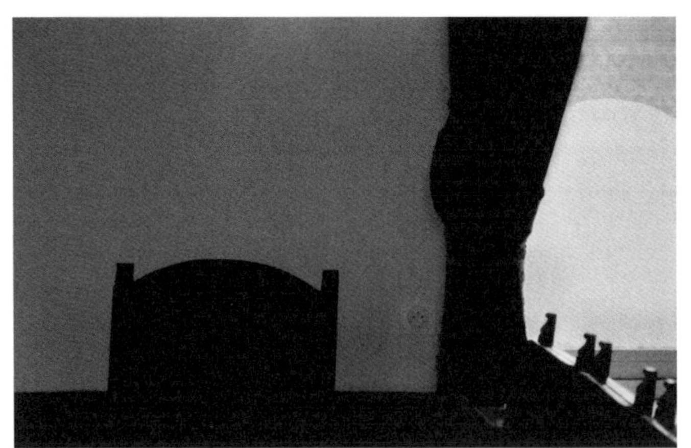

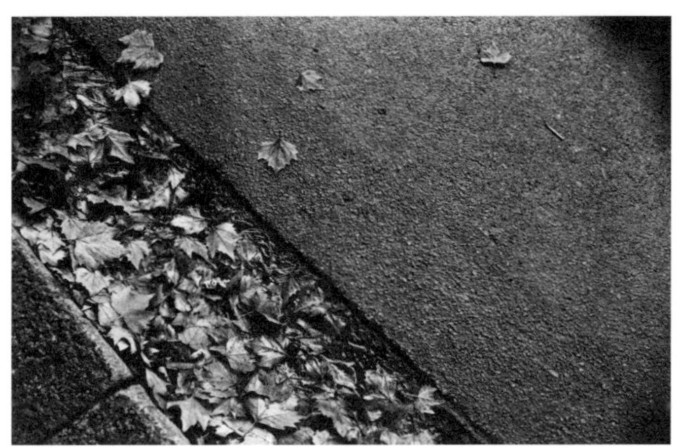

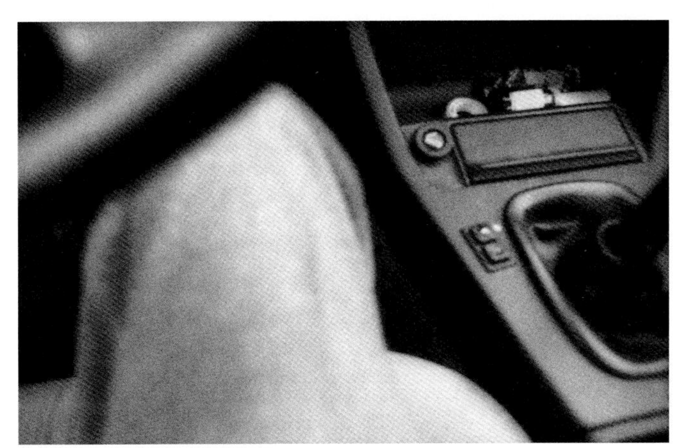

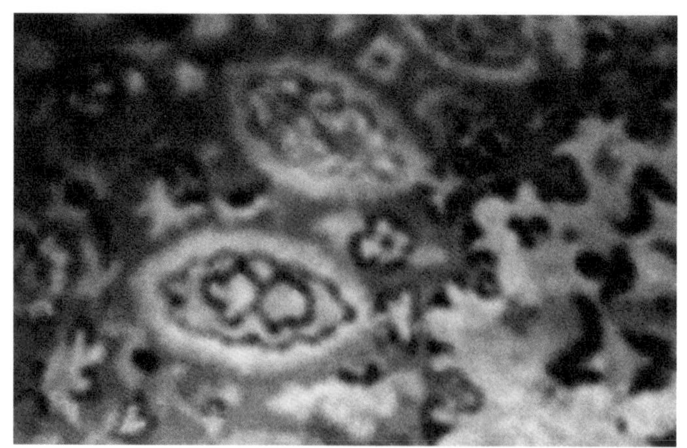

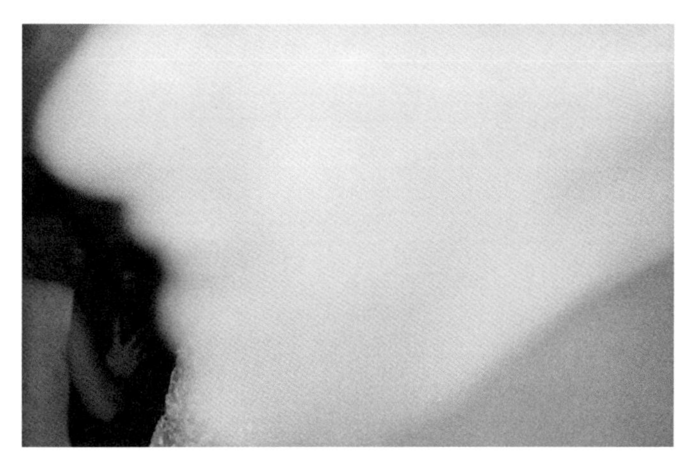

Dominique Somers' work *00A* consists of a remarkable compilation of found images. The title of the series refers to the starting-point markings printed between the sprocket holes on the leader of a 35-mm photographic film. Somers has been collecting the first, automatic exposures made on this *00A* frame of the negative strip for years. They are the result of a photographic practice that in today's digital age has almost become a form of archaeology: when positioning a roll of analogue film in the camera, one has to release the shutter a few times and wind a couple of frames forward to reach the starting position *(1A)* of the unexposed part of the spooled film. It is precisely these throwaway shots, made while loading the camera before the real work begins, that Somers has appropriated. When processing the found photo rolls in their black cassettes she is only interested in the first, "blind" exposures. Her mode of operation can be described as photography without a photographer. Somers inverts the usual procedure, cuts away what the photographer intended to record in a deliberate aesthetical gesture and keeps what he or she considered unworthy of a single glance. She gives this "failed" exposure a second life and a new meaning. Strolling in her archive of found images, the artist trusts in the poetry of the unexpected find: her gaze lights up the unconscious image and lends it autonomy. By assembling hundreds of these involuntary exposures, Somers generates a wonderful and enigmatic universe of technical images.

The black-and-white images that are part of this series can by no means be read as photorealistic windows on the world. Rather, they are opaque screens filled with white noise that hinder a clear view of reality. The *00A* exposures are the result of an uncontrolled mechanical process, of looking without an "I", of optical scanning detached from the human eye. The viewing machine in free fall has seen everything but recognized nothing; it seems hypersensitive to textures and unhindered by meaning, codes or rhetoric. Photography is rarely abstraction in its purest sense because it always depicts certain circumstances in the world (just as the sound of words always means something). The photo presents a trace of that state of affairs in front of the lens at the moment of exposure. But these chance encounters between a strip of film and all kinds of unrecognizable objects, capricious shadows and banal details such as randomly cropped crosswalks and floor tiles, shoes and automobile wheels, release cables and the occasional bare arm seem extraordinarily strange, unreal even. Every element of the photographic apparatus does what it is meant to do. Lens, shutter speed and light-sensitive material register the surface of the world, whether oblique or at a slant, extremely close or too far away, over- or underexposed, but without an operator the camera is blind, a myopic *dispositif* without intention or insight. Precisely this failure of photographic representation triggers Somers' attention. For her, every artistic interaction with the medium of photography begins with the mistake, the accident, the stuttering of the image. She herself refers to it in terms of Samuel Beckett's well-known phrase: *Ever tried. Ever failed. No matter. Try again. Fail again. Fail better*.

The *00A* image is given, not made. It is the antipode of the naïve, redundant photography of amateurs and journalists, the users of 35-mm cameras. As a series, *00A* investigates the boundaries of the technical and conceptual identity of photography. It plays with automatism and chance, both characteristic of the photographic exposure process. By consistently sticking to her method Somers builds up a treasure trove of unexpected images. The forensic quality, graphic patterns and grainy mosaics in *00A* evoke photograms as defined by Bauhaus artist Laszlo Moholy-Nagy: *abstract seeing by means of direct records of forms produced by light.* The unanticipated scenes and surprising perspectives of these images also recall the Surrealists' *écriture automatique.* André Breton called the camera *un instrument aveugle.* Exactly because the machine is detached from human consciousness, it is capable of revealing the enigmatic character of reality. In the *00A* series, the world appears in a chaotic manner and crumbled into crude particles, cut off from the categories of time and space.
Chance also produced masterpieces in Man Ray's case. Asked about his favourite photograph, Man Ray replied: *l'instantané fortuit d'une ombre,* an accidental passage between two portrait shots of a girl on the beach when the camera toppled over and accidently registered a shadow. If the camera operates independently of the countless conscious decisions relating to point of view – framing – exposure time and depth of field – photography is reduced to its essence: a mechanical registration method in which light is inscribed on a light-sensitive carrier and in a chemical emulsion of silver salts – without human intervention. The automatic exposure thus reveals what usually remains concealed in "transparent" snapshots: something of the substance of the medium, apart from its subject. In a beautiful

phenomenological analysis of the earliest images recorded by Nicéphore Nièpce on the glass of a camera obscura in 1822, Hubert Damisch remarks the appearance *of a photographic substance distinct from subject matter.* In the *00A* images, something of the conditions of the production of images by the technical apparatus also becomes visible. That which precedes depiction. The degree zero of the photo. The materiality of the support, the grainy texture, the absence of perspective, distortions particular to the lens and the camera's construction, and the program of the "black box" itself. But penetrating to the essence of photography at the same time destroys its functionality: the image becomes entirely abstract. It represents nothing but the photographic process itself. In a single tautological movement the gaze turns on itself. This particular form of photographic abstraction is part of the plastic material with which Somers works. In the repetition of hundreds of *00A* images she insists on another way of looking, on sensitivity to sculpting with light and white noise, attention to detail, on capturing the unsteady, fragile appearance of motifs that lose all specificity and threaten to dissolve into the material of the image itself.

According to the Prague philosopher Vilèm Flusser, the experimental photographer plays *against* the apparatus as long as he or she makes its automatic programming subordinate to human intentions. Adversely, *00A* exposes the rigid program of the "black box" that unintentionally makes all of its possibilities a reality and functions without the photographer's controlling quest for meaningful motifs. But in the slow, attentive process of collecting, selecting, editing and remixing of this photographic "waste material", a liberating, ludic power of the imagination eventually takes over: this is something that is not pre-programmed by the apparatus.

Inge Henneman

- Hubert Damisch, "Five Notes for a Phenomenology of the Photographic Image," *October,* no. 5 (1978); first French edition in *L'Arc,* 1963.
- Dirk Lauwaert, "Het Beeld dat Alles prijsgeeft (omdat het Niets heeft gezien)," in *Lichtpapier: Teksten over fotografie,* Bibliotheek van de Fotografie 3, FotoMuseum Provincie Antwerpen and Nederlands fotomuseum, 2007, pp. 141–50.
- Man Ray, *La Photographie n'est pas l'art,* Editions GLM, 1937.
- Vilèm Flusser, *Een filosofie van de fotografie,* Uitgeverij IJzer, 2007.

APE#057
Dominique Somers
00A

ISBN 9789490800383
www.artpapereditions.org
www.dominiquesomers.com
First edition of 500 copies

Graphic design:
Studio Jurgen Maelfeyt
Text: Inge Henneman
Translation: Irene Schaudies
Printing: Graphius, Ghent
Distribution: Idea Books,
www.ideabooks.nl

This publication is financially supported by the Flemish Community and School of Arts Ghent / UGent. It is made within the context of the doctoral research project entitled *Everything That Shines Sees*.

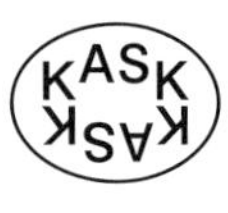

HoGent

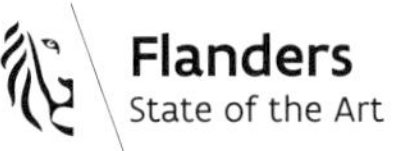